making

printed in the USA • published by Madder

MW00668839

Handspun fun by Kirsten Kapur on Nash Island, Maine.

Ever since I was little, I have loved animals. When I was about six years old I remember begging my parents, with tears in my eyes, to buy me a puppy at the pet store. We compromised with a goldfish, which sadly did not live long. Eventually, when I was ten I got my first kitten, white with caramel spots, and named him Buttons. He was a frisky little thing who would attack our legs if left bare under the dinner table. Oh, but I did not care—I adored him.

Now I am on the other end of this question: "Mama can I get a dog, a donkey, a draft horse, a pony, some goats, oh—and some sheep?" asks Imogen. Sigrid nods in agreement. If she were talking more, I definitely think she would also ask for a few extra cats (preferrably ones that like to be hugged). I do wish my husband and I could say yes to living with a lot more animals! And perhaps someday we may, but for now we will stick with our three cats and varying numbers of chickens

This past year, I was fortunate to visit with some people who have said yes and are living with animals as one of the center points of their lives. Ashley Yousling, Amanda Blake Soule, and Tammy White are three women I had the great pleasure of visiting at their homesteads. These ladies' dedication to raising animals amazes me, for the work they and their families do is hard and endless. The rewards, however, bring rich experiences and useful products such as eggs, honey, meat, and yarn which they use and share with their local community.

Not all of us can (or want to) homestead, but I think many of us can appreciate the joys that animals bring to our lives. Fauna can be comforting companions and therapeutic in a way that nothing else can heal. They can teach us to respect the wild nature in us all. Animals are beautiful and quirky and mysterious. And ever so importantly, they provide us with materials to make! Yarn, thread, and fabric to name a few.

Fauna can also give us unexpected moments of wonder, as I experienced on a trip this past summer to Nash Island with Mary Jane Mucklestone. A treasured day, being a part of this sheep shearing—I hope always to remember. I held my first lamb with tears in my eyes, but different than those of a six year old in a pet store. I was moved by the magical feeling of embracing such a soft, little, untamed beauty.

After these travels, I was left with many warm memories which helped to fuel the work that followed: bringing this issue, No. 2 / FAUNA, to life. Of course, these pages would not be what they are without the contributions of the skillful designers and crafts people who have created some of the sweetest projects for this issue of *Making*. I am so grateful!

FAUNA is a tribute to the various creatures that intrigue and inspire us, either at our homes or in the wild. These pages (and there are so many more compared to this past spring!) are chock full of goodness. I do hope you will find months of making here.

Carrie Bostick Hoge / Editor

connect
online: www.makingzine.com
email: hello@makingzine.com

3

HANDWORK
9-11, 146
Covered Journal
cross-stitching & sewing by Lori Ann Graham

12-15
Woolly Tattoo Pillow
embroidery by Tif Fussell

145
Simple Pillow
knit pattern by Carrie Bostick Hoge

16-17, 146
Bee Embroidery & Tote
embroidery & sewing by Beatrice Perron Dahlen

BEAUTY & UTILITY
19-21
Rosa Sachets
natural dyeing, embroidery, and sewing
by Kristine Vejar

22-27
Wool + Wax Tote
sewn tote by Anna Graham

28-31
Scales Wallhanging Quilt
quilting & embroidery by Carolyn Friedlander

HANDSPUN
34-35, 102-103
Orchard Grass Stole
knit pattern by Ashley Yousling

36-37, 104-106
Camellia Tank
knit pattern by Karen Templer

38-41
Drop Spindle Spinning
tutorial by Casey Ryder

HOME
43
Brandy Milk Punch
cocktail recipe by Trey Hughes

44-47, 146, 152
Caramelized Fig Pear-Ginger Pie
recipe by Tammy White

48-49
Coloring Sheets
drawings by Nicole Dupuis

HOMESTEAD
51-57
East & West
a conversation between Amanda Blake Soule
and Ashley Yousling

EXPLORE
59-63
Nash Island Sheep Shearing
essay by Mary Jane Mucklestone

64-65
Swatch Diaries
by Carrie Bostick Hoge

KIDS
67, 107-108
Doe Cap
knit pattern by Jenny Gordy

5, 68-70, 148-149
Squirrel
sewing by Grainline Studio

71-73, 150
Fox Tooth Fairy Pillow
sewing by Sanae Ishida

74-76, 147, 150
Woodland Finger Puppets
sewing & embroidery by Mollie Johanson

76-77, 109-112
Butterfly & Cocoon
knit pattern by Susan B. Anderson

78-79
Narwhals & Friends
needle felting by Kim Hamlin

SEA & SHORE
81, 113-114
Sea Urchin Treasure Bag
knit pattern by Mary Jane Mucklestone

82-83, 115-118
Byssus Cocoon
knit pattern by Bristol Ivy

84-85, 118-120
Open Waters Shawl
knit pattern by Melanie Berg

86-87, 120-121
Open Waters Cowl
knit pattern by Melanie Berg

88, 122-124
Arctic Coat
knit pattern by Carrie Bostick Hoge

89, 125
Arctic Cowl
knit pattern by Carrie Bostick Hoge

FOREST & FIELD
91, 125-126
Wild Feather Mitts
knit pattern by Cecily Glowik MacDonald

5, 92-93, 127-132
Stag Head Pullover
knit pattern by Norah Gaughan

94-95, 132-134
Throstle Shawl
knit pattern by Bristol Ivy

96-97, 141-143
Nyla Hat
crochet pattern by Cal Patch

98-99, 135-140
Nepali Bird Vest
knit pattern by Carol Sunday

100-101, 143-144
Town-O Cap
knit pattern by Beatrice Perron Dahlen

151-152
Abbreviations & Techniques

table of contents

All photographs by Carrie Bostick Hoge
except when otherwise noted.

Chapter Illustrations by Emily Walker.

© 2016 madder

All rights reserved. No part of this publication may be
reproduced or transmitted in any form or by any means,
electronic, mechanical, photocopying, recording, or otherwise, without prior written permission from the publisher.

a
verb
for
keeping
warm

knit, sew, dye

www.averbforkeepingwarm.com

HANDWORK

Covered Journal
by Lori Ann Graham

Covered Journal with Cross–Stitch
by Lori Ann Graham

I truly believe the enjoyment that can be found in journal keeping begins first with finding your "style." Ask yourself, do you like to write a lot? Perhaps choose a book with lined paper. If adding drawings is an interest, blank pages would work best. And if your journaling spirit is also a bit "magpie," then a sewn cover might be what is needed. A fabric cover can fasten closed (in a myriad of ways) keeping treasures safe inside. The book flaps will conveniently hold nature finds: a feather, butterfly wings, even bits of sheeps' wool discovered on a shrub while walking in the highlands (or closer to home), can be tucked inside.

A question sometimes asked is "how to begin a journal?" or "how to keep it up?" or anxiously "I'm afraid I'll mess it up." The intentional process of journaling can be approached in so many different ways, there really is no right or wrong. Anything that inspires can be the subject of your book.

Here is my best secret: write, draw, and save what you want to remember. When you record with your heart, you'll have a book to cherish.

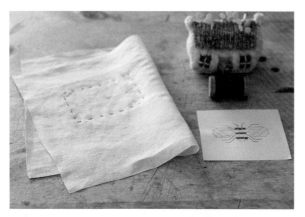
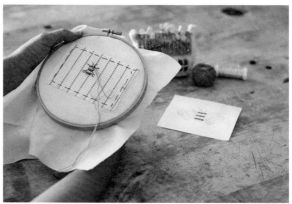

Photographs by Lori Ann Graham

Supplies

- ½ yard [45.75 cm] of fabric (linen or cotton works best)
- Waste canvas (I've used 14 count, but any size will work)
- Embroidery hoop
- Crewel needles
- Embroidery thread in chosen colors
- Basting thread / sewing thread
- Chart
- Scissors
- Pins
- 2 safety pins
- Tweezers or needle-nose pliers
- 36" [91.5 cm] of shoestring leather or ribbon
- Knitting needle or other narrow and sharp tool for turning
- Blank book (I use artist sketch books sized 5½" x 8½" [14 cm x 21.5 cm], although any size may be used and fabric size can adjust accordingly)

Optional

- Sewing machine
- Needle threader
- Button

Cross-stitch with waste canvas

Cut four rectangles from fabric: two in size 16" x 10" [41 x 25.5 cm] and two in size 10" x 8" [25.5 x 20.5 cm].

Make a copy of the bee design (two templates provided on page 146, use simpler version if desired).

Center bee on the front of one of the large rectangles, determining placement by wrapping the fabric around the blank book.

Pin waste canvas in place, making sure it's straight. Using sewing thread, baste all the way around the edges of the waste canvas.

Using 3 strands of DMC thread, follow the chart. Cross-stitch the bee first, then backstitch the wings. When all stitching is complete, carefully remove basting thread and trim waste canvas closely to stitching.

Keeping a hand on the cross-stitching (to support the stitches), use tweezers or needle nose pliers to gently, but firmly, pull out waste canvas threads, one at a time.

Journal Cover

Place ribbon or leather at the edge of the center middle of the right side (see photo for placement). Fold the two smaller rectangle pieces in half lengthwise and place one on each edge of large rectangle.

Place the second large rectangle face down, so the large rectangles are right-side together. Pin all the way around, leaving a 2½" [6.5 cm] opening at the bottom. Be sure to do this at the center and not at the side rectangles. I have used safety pins to designate where.

Sew through all layers, all the way around by hand or with a machine, using a 1" [2.5 cm] seam allowance—taking care not to catch the ribbon (except at the front seam where it is pinned)—starting and stopping at the safety pins.

Trim corners, trim seam to ½" [1.25 cm].

Turn right side out. At this point it's good to check for fit, depending how snug you'd like your cover. I like mine a little on the looser side to allow for the ever-expanding journal pages.

Using a knitting needle or other pointy tool, gently push out the corners.

Press. Slip stitch opening closed.

Optional: With a complimentary or contrasting thread, make a running stitch by hand or a top stitch with a machine, around the entire outside edge.

Wrap ribbon around to close. (A button may be added to anchor the ribbon around).

Gather your journaling supplies and begin recording!

Lori is a photographer, traveler, and knitter living in the central coast of California.
Instagram: loritimesfive

Woolly Tattoo Pillow
by Tif Fussell

Spiffy Beetle and His Flora Woolly Tattoo
by Tif Fussell

Many moons ago I learnt to embroider. It made my crafty soul sing, but alas, I was unable to find a way to incorporate it into my making. Then one fine recent day I stumbled upon the idea of using wool. How marvelous it was, for I got to stitch, the stitches got to be chunky or not and they got to be rustic or not depending on the type of yarn I chose. The term "woolly tattoo" came from my thoughts for stitching onto areas of handmade knitted garments or thrifted finds, where one would typically place a real tattoo on the body. With just a few different stitches, a lovely palette of yarns, it was possible to create detailed "tattoos," simplistic in their beginnings, becoming rather more so by the end. I do so hope you will enjoy making this spiffy Beetle and his Flora, taking the time to slow down the world around and immerse yourself into the calming world of woolly tattoo-ing.

Notes
When stitching into a knitted fabric be sure to not pull too tight nor too loose. If you are unsure and this is your first time placing embroidery on a flexible knitted fabric you may wish to practice on the swatch you created for the cushion cover.

All measurements are approximate; do not fret trying to get your Beetle and his Flora to exact size. You can go bigger or smaller if you choose.

Consider embroidering before finishing the seams of the Simple Pillow (see page 145). Additionally, placing a large piece of cardboard between the two layers can help. Also check the underside of your work from time to time; occasionally things can get a little loopy under there!

I start with my yarn knotted and pull it carefully up through a knitted stitch in the cushion cover so it is anchored. I finish off either by tying a small knot or weaving under stitches on the reverse. Best to not have too long a piece of yarn to work with, as it can start to fray with all the to-ing and fro-ing.

My style of woolly tattooing is very organic and the stitches are not evenly executed, thus creating a more freeform feel for the finished piece. If you are happy to embrace this way of stitching you will likely be more delighted with the outcome of your piece!

Be careful not to distort the knitted cushion fabric. You need to take a delicate approach to the stitching so the two layers may be harmonious rather than in distress.

And lastly, do read all the way through before you begin. I have broken the instructions up into how each separate element is created, and then explain at the end how I build up the overall design.

Supplies
• Small scissors
• Sharp pointed tapestry needles (with large eyes)
• Regular cotton sewing thread (for outlining beetle)
For Flora:
• Wool yarn, single- or double-ply in fingering and worsted weights in 4 complimentary colors.
For Beetle:
• Wool yarn, single-or double-ply in fingering weight in 2 similar colors and 1 contrast. (A yarn with a bit of texture would work brilliantly.)

Stitches

Flora: lazy daisy stitch, bullion stitch
Beetle: lazy daisy stitch, couching stitch, chain stitch
(If new to embroidery, fret not! YouTube is a great resource for learning, and the Stitch Encyclopedia of Embroidery by Chronicle books is also a goodie.)

Woolly Tattooing

(See template illustrations pages 14–15.)
The big flower
Approximately 3" x 3½" [7.5 cm x 9 cm]
Use either worsted weight yarn (or fingering held double) to create the petals and a smooth fingering yarn (not held double) for the bullion middle.

The flower is made up of an inner ring, a middle ring, and an outer ring of lazy daisy stitches. Starting with the inner ring, create an oval of lazy daisy stitches, leaving a space in the center for the bullion stitches. Change colors, add a middle ring, change colors again and add an outer ring of stitches. For the center of the flower, create 'spokes' of bullion stitches like a bicycle wheel.

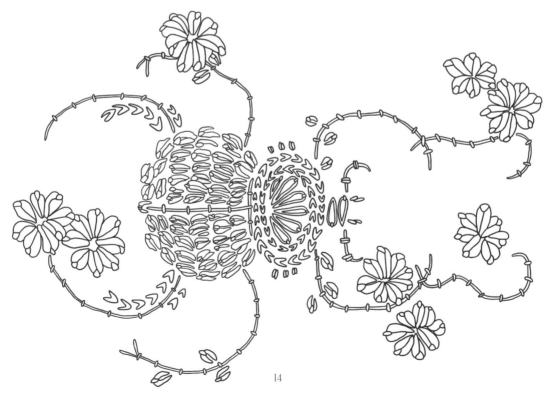

The small flower
Approximately 1" [2.5 cm]
Using the same yarn from the inner ring of the big flower, stitch a circle of lazy daisy stitches close together, being sure not to leave any space in the center.

The beetle
Approximately 3½" x 2½" [9 cm x 6.25 cm], excluding legs
Make a copy of the beetle body template, pin in place and transfer shape using running stitch and cotton thread. (Be sure to leave enough fabric space at the top and below to fit his legs in.) With chosen fingering weight yarn held double, start filling in the bottom half of his body with lazy daisy stitches, covering the outline thread as you go. Next outline the top half of the body with two rows of chain stitch, work the outside row first, again being sure to cover the temporary outline thread, then come back the other way, creating an inner row of chain stitches. Then come up with your needle in the middle where the top half joins the bottom half of the body. From here, spiral out filling the space with big oversized lazy daisy stitches, placed close together.

The legs are created freeform using couching stitch. Looking at the illustration and the photos for inspiration, tackle each pair of legs at a time. To make the curves, be sure to leave enough slack yarn so the couching stitch does not become too tight as you begin stitching it down in place. (This may be a good stitch to practice on a spare piece of knitted fabric first.) As you can see, I have placed a few lazy daisy stitches on some parts of the legs and also on the bottom legs a little row of chain stitching along the inside. Get creative with the legs: think a little frilly and all will be good. Change to the second fingering weight color, again held double, and highlight areas on the beetle: a sprinkling on the body, along the couching legs and a few dashes in the top half of his body too. Finally, using your contrast color yarn, create a T shape with 2 couching stitches on his body, and also a small bit of couching and 2 lazy daisy stitches help create his antenna bits.

Building the woolly tattoo design
Start in the bottom right hand area of the cushion cover and stitch an L shape consisting of 6 large flowers. Next add clusters of small flowers, scattering them around and within the shape of large flowers. Stop from time to time and take a look. Sometimes we have to step away from the woolly blinging to see what is missing or, indeed, if all is good just as it is. Proceed to stitching your beetle in the open space left and festoon him with a light sprinkling of small flowers and voila! Your woolly tattoo is complete.

Illustrations by Meg Fussell
Instagram: prideofmice

Tif is a woolly tattoo artist living in WA.
Instagram: dottieangel / #woollytattoo

Bee Tote
by Beatrice Perron Dahlen

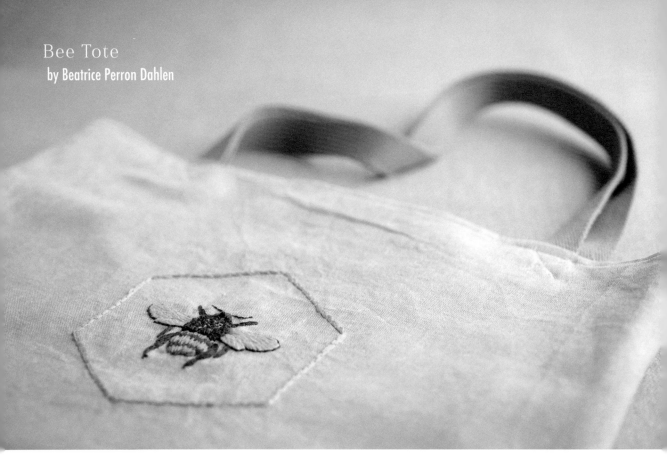

Embroidered Bee Tote
by Beatrice Perron Dahlen

I've long had a forced affinity for bees. Being named "Bea," I've gotten many bee gifts over the years. I suppose it's stuck, and in my adult years I've become fascinated by bees and their intelligence. The Bee Tote marries my love of embroidery, fascination with bees, beauty, and function.

Supplies
For Bag:
• ½ yard [45.75 cm] of prewashed 44" [111.75 cm] wide fabric (pictured in Robert Kaufman Linen Blend) or piece of fabric 18" [45.75 cm] wide and double desired depth
• ½ yard [45.75 cm] of prewashed 44" [111.75 cm] wide lining fabric (pictured lined with white linen) or piece of fabric 18" [45.75 cm] wide and double desired depth
• 1½ yards [137.25 cm] of cotton webbing, cut into two pieces
• Matching thread

For Embroidery:
• Tracing paper
• Insect template
• Ballpoint pen
• Embroidery thread
• Embroidery needle
• Embroidery hoop

Embroidery
Make a photo copy of the bee template (See page 146). Place the tracing paper on top of the pre-washed fabric. Place the bee template on top of this where you would like your embroidery to be. Using the ballpoint pen, trace over the image to transfer the template to the fabric. Place your fabric in the embroidery hoop and stitch away! Stitches used in bee: French knot and satin for the body, winged outlined with back stitch and filled in with satin stitch.

Trace a hexagon around your bee and using the back stitch, stitch over the line, making a honey-comb around the bee.

Tote

1. With RS facing (the side with your completed embroidery), fold long sides of fabric in half so that the two short sides of the fabric meet (fold is at the bottom). Pin the two sides of the fabric, leaving the top open. Stitch up each side with a ½" [1.25 cm] seam allowance. Reinforce with a second seam and/or zig zag stitch.

2. Repeat with lining fabric.

3. Box the corners by finding the center line of the bottom and pressing it together with the side seam, one corner at a time. Use a ruler to measure 3" from the tip. Pin and then cut this triangle off on both corners of both tote and lining fabric (4 corners). Sew open edge with a ½" [1.25 cm] seam allowance and reinforce seam. Repeat for all four corners. Press.

4. Press the tops of each fabric piece over 1½" [3.75 cm] toward the wrong side of the fabric.

5. Now the liner should have seams exposed on the outside of the bag, while the bag has seams facing in so that the embroidery is visible.

6. Pin the raw end of cotton webbing onto the tote liner about 3" [7.5 cm] from the seam on each side of the handle. Repeat on the other side for the second handle.

7. Slide the liner into the bag, pinning the top edges together.

8. Stitch an "X" through the tote, handle and liner, four times.

9. Top stitch the top of the bag, all the way around about ¼" [.75 cm] from top edge.

Bea is an artist, photographer, and knitwear designer based in Portland, ME.
www.threadandladle.com Instagram: threadandladle

BEAUTY & UTILITY

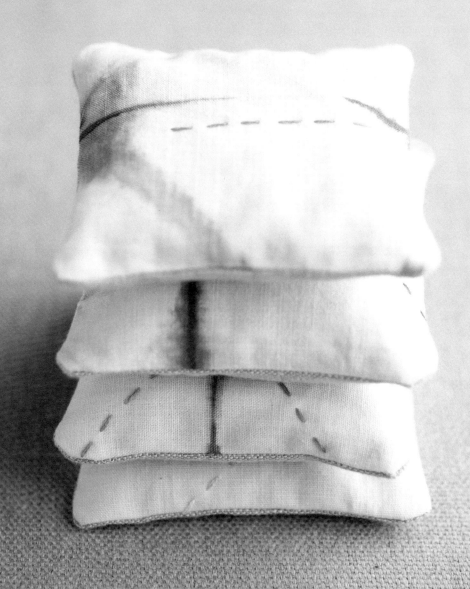

Rosa Sachets
by Kristine Vejar

Cochineal is one of the most magical and interesting dyes commonly used in the natural dyeing process. Throughout the desert regions of California, Arizona, Mexico, and Central and South America, there grows a cactus named Opuntia (also commonly called nopal). It has thick, succulent paddles, and is a common ingredient in Mexican cuisine. If you look closely at a nopal cactus sometimes there is a white furry growth. This is an insect named cochineal. If left to roost, the cochineal, similar to an aphid, will take the nutrients from the plant and the cactus will eventually die. So cochineal is typically removed from the cactus. Sometimes when it is removed it is kept, dried, and used as a dye. For as long as we know, people in Mexico, and Central and South America have used cochineal as the primary way to achieve pink. Through shifting the pH of the water in the dyebath, colors from red to purple can also be achieved.

When Carrie announced the theme for *Making* Fall 2016 as Fauna, I instantly thought of cochineal and wanted to use it as the central dye and color for this project. Then, I thought of other fauna, which are best kept at bay, away from our stashes of yarn and fabric, like moths, and thought—I'll make sachets!

To create the pattern on the fabric used for the sachets, I ground cochineal and added it to a pot of water. I pleated and clamped the fabric and then put it in the dyebath. Once I was done dyeing the fabric, I removed the clamps. All the lines you see with the color pink are the areas exposed to the dye, and all of the white, undyed areas were under pressure due to the clamps, making it impossible for the dye to reach the cloth. I always like to add a bit of simple embroidery, to create a bit of texture, and to add a special hand-made detail.

Rosa Sachet kits are available through www.averbforkeepingwarm.com & www.makingzine.com. Or you can learn to dye with cochineal through reading *The Modern Natural Dyer*.

Kristine is the owner of A Verb for Keeping Warm in Oakland, CA. She is the author of The Modern Natural Dyer. *www.averbforkeepingwarm.com Instagram: avfkw*

Finished size
4" x 4" [10.25 cm x 10.25 cm]

Supplies
- Embroidery needle
- Cochineal dyed DMC floss
- 5" x 5" [12.75 cm x 12.75 cm] square of cochineal dyed fabric
- 5" x 5" [12.75 cm x 12.75 cm] square of natural linen fabric
- Approx ½ cup blend of lavender, rosemary, and cedar chips

Sachets
1. Using three strands of DMC floss, add a line or two of running stitch across the dyed fabric.

2. Place dyed fabric and linen fabric right sides together. Using a running stitch, stitch two fabrics together ½" [1.25 cm] from the edge. Leave a 2" [5 cm] gap in your stitching on one of the four sides.

3. Use this gap to pull the sachet right-side out.

4. Stuff the sachet with lavender, rosemary, and/or cedar wood chips.

5. Stitch the sachet closed using a blind stitch.

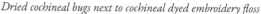

Dried cochineal bugs next to cochineal dyed embroidery floss

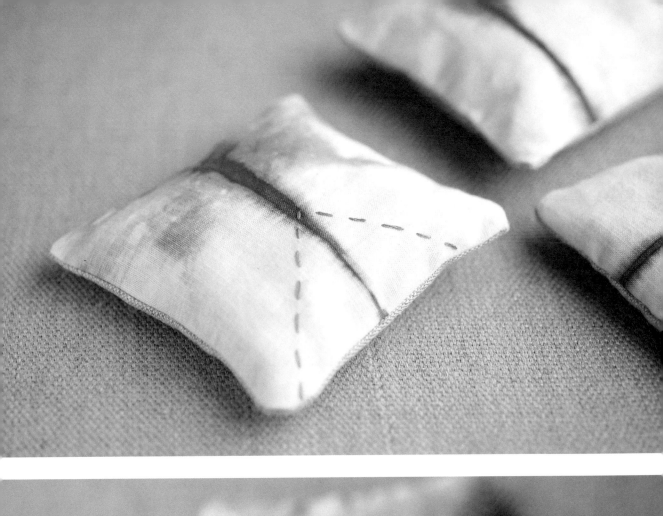

Wool + Wax Tote
by Anna Graham

Wool + Wax Tote
Anna Graham

A classic tote using wool fabric and waxed canvas. This simple and elegant tote will look great with anything and will keep your must-have essentials close at hand. A divided front pocket is perfect for stashing keys and a phone.

Finished Size
- 15" [38 cm] tall, 13" [33 cm] wide and 3" [7.5 cm] deep

Skill level: Advanced beginner

Supplies
- Fabric requirements based on 44" [111.75 cm] wide fabric
- ¾ yard [68.5 cm] exterior fabric
- 1 yard [91.5 cm] non-directional lining fabric
- ½ yard [45.75 cm] contrasting bottom fabric
- 2¼ yards [205.75 cm] fusible woven interfacing (Pellon SF101 – 20" [50.75 cm] wide)
- (2) 1" [2.5 cm] wide leather handles or cotton webbing, 28" [71 cm] long
- Optional: (3) 8-9 mm double cap rivets

Recommended Fabrics: Waxed canvas for contrast bottom. Cotton or blended canvas, denim, wool, twill, home dec for Exterior and Lining.

A few tips for working with waxed canvas:
- Double stitch within the seam allowance for extra durability. I sew an additional row of stitching ⅛" [.5 cm] away from the actual seam (but within seam allowance) for reinforcement.
- A Teflon foot might be helpful so the waxed canvas doesn't stick as it's being fed through your machine.
- Pin holes will be visible. Instead, pin within the seam allowance or use binder clips.
- Finger press seams. If you have to iron, use a low heat setting and no steam. Cover with pressing cloth.

Additional supplies and tools
- Polyester thread
- Chalk or water-soluble pen
- Cutting mat
- Ruler
- Rotary cutter
- Turning tool
- Size 14 or 16 denim needle

Notes
- ½" [1.25 cm] seam allowance throughout, unless otherwise noted.
- ¼" [.75 cm] seam allowance for basting.
- Make sure to backstitch at beginning and end of each seam to secure stitches.
- Topstitch ⅛" [.5 cm] away from edges or seams.
- Use a longer stitch length when topstitching (3.0mm) for even and smooth stitches.
- To find center, finger-press in half and mark within seam allowance.

RST=right sides together, WST=wrong sides together

Cut from Exterior Fabric:
- (2) 12" [30.5 cm] tall x 17" [43.25 cm] wide Exterior Main
- (1) 9" [22.75 cm] tall x 17" [43.25 cm] wide Front Exterior Pocket

Cut from Lining Fabric:
- (1) 34" [86.25 cm] tall x 17" [43.25 cm] wide Lining Main
- (1) 9" [22.75 cm] tall x 17" [43.25 cm] wide Front Exterior Pocket
- (2) 7" [17.75 cm] tall x 10" [25.5 cm] wide Slip Pocket

Cut from Contrast Bottom Fabric:
(1) 12" [30.5 cm] tall x 17" [43.5 cm] wide Contrast Bottom

Cut from Fusible Woven Interfacing:
- (2) 12" [30.5 cm] tall x 17" [43.25 cm] wide Exterior Main
- (1) 9" [22.75 cm] tall x 17" [43.25 cm] wide Front Exterior Pocket
- (1) 34" [86.25 cm] tall x 17" [43.25 cm] wide Lining Main
- (1) 7" [17.75 cm] tall x 10" [25.5 cm] wide Slip Pocket

Fuse interfacing
- Fuse interfacing to wrong side of Exterior Main pieces and Front Exterior Pocket exterior fabric.
- Fuse interfacing to wrong side of Lining Main fabric and Slip Pocket piece.

Note: Because waxed canvas is sturdy there is no need to add interfacing.

Make front Exterior pocket
1. Place Front Exterior Pocket lining and exterior fabrics RST and pin along one long edge. Sew.

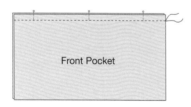

2. Position fabrics WST and press. Topstitch along the pressed edge. Sew additional row of topstitching ¼" [.75 cm] below previous topstitching.

3. With one Exterior Main right side up, place assembled pocket on top (exterior facing up), aligning to bottom and side edges. Baste in place along pocket sides and bottom.

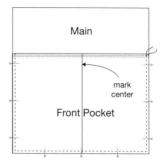

4. With chalk or a water-soluble pen, mark a vertical line centered on front pocket. Sew ⅛" [.5 cm] from marked line beginning at bottom edge of pocket, pivoting and stitching 2-3 stitches along the finished pocket's top edge and pivoting again to sew down the other side of the marked line. The pocket will now be divided in two. Set aside.

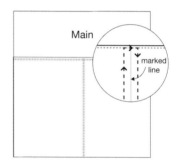

Assemble Exterior
1. Fold Contrast Bottom in half RST matching 17" [43.25 cm] edges. Using a clear ruler mark a rectangle 1½" [3.75 cm] wide by 1" [2.5 cm] tall in each corner at the bottom fold. Cut out each corner along marked rectangle.

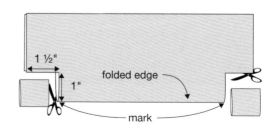

2. With chalk or a water-soluble pen, mark a line within the seam allowance at the bottom fold on both sides of the Contrast Bottom. Unfold Contrast Bottom.

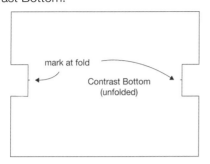

3. Place bottom (bottom of Front Exterior Pocket) 17" [43.25 cm] edge of assembled front exterior RST with one 17" [43.25 cm] edge of Contrast Bottom. Pin in place and sew. Press seam allowance toward Contrast Bottom.

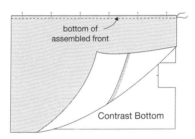

4. Topstitch along seam on Contrast Bottom.

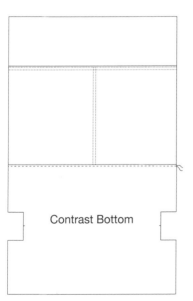

5. Repeat Steps 3-4 for assembled back exterior, aligning one 17" [43.25 cm] edge of remaining Exterior Main with the opposite 17" [43.25 cm] edge of Contrast Bottom. The completed exterior will look like this:

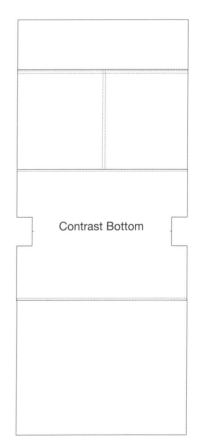

6. Fold assembled exterior in half RST. Pin and sew both side seams. Press seam allowance toward tote front.
Tip: Be sure to match the contrast bottom seams along each side of tote.

7. To sew corner seam, reach inside tote and pinch bottom corner together. Align bottom marking to its corresponding side seam. Pin and sew.

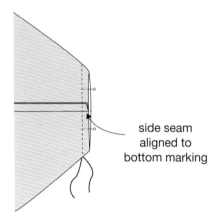

side seam
aligned to
bottom marking

8. Repeat Step 7 for other tote corner.

9. Turn tote right side out.

10. Optional: Set rivets on top edge of pocket on the front Exterior Main near both side seams and one centered on pocket's sewn divider.

Make lining
1. Place Slip Pocket pieces RST. Sew along all edges leaving a 3" [7.5 cm] opening along bottom 10" [25.5 cm] edge. Clip corners and turn right side out through opening. Use turning tool to push out corners. Press and tuck in raw edges of the opening.

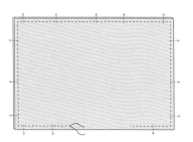

2. Topstitch along top edge of pocket. (Opening will be sewn closed in Step 3.) Sew additional row of topstitching ¼" [.75 cm] below previous topstitching.

3. Center pocket 4½" [11.5 cm] down from one 17" [43.25 cm] lining edge. Pin in place.

4. Topstitch along Slip Pocket sides and bottom, starting and ending with a triangle in each upper corner for reinforcement.

5. With chalk or a water-soluble pen, mark vertical line(s) on Slip Pocket as desired to divide pocket into sections. Sew on marked line(s) beginning at bottom edge of pocket remembering to backstitch at both beginning and end of each line.

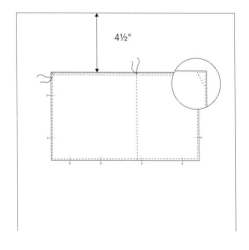

4½"

6. Fold assembled lining in half RST, matching 17" [43.25 cm] edges. Using a clear ruler mark a rectangle 1½" [3.75 cm] wide by 1" [2.5 cm] tall in each corner at the bottom fold. Cut out each corner along marked rectangle.

7. With chalk or a water-soluble pen, mark a line within the seam allowance at the fold just as in 'Assemble Exterior' Step 2.

8. Sew both side seams, leaving an 8-9" [20-23 cm] opening on one side for turning later. Press seams open (including those at opening left for turning).

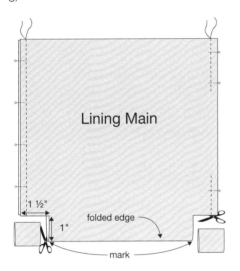

9. Sew tote corner seams as in Step 7 from "Assemble exterior". Trim seam allowance to ¼" [.75 cm]. Set completed lining aside.

Complete tote
1. Mark center on tote exterior front, make a mark 2½" [6.25 cm] on both sides of the center mark. Repeat for Exterior back.

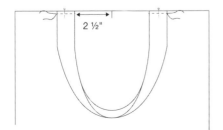

2. Align inner edge of handle to 2½" [6.25 cm] marking, aligning short edge of handle to raw edge of tote top. Be careful not to twist the Handle. Pin handle in place. Baste. Repeat for remaining handle and exterior back.

3. Place assembled exterior into assembled lining RST, aligning side seams. Handles will be facing down into the tote in between exterior and lining. Interior Pocket will be RST with tote's exterior back. Pin, then sew along top open edge.

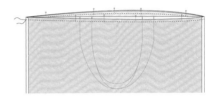

4. Turn right side out through opening in lining. Tuck in raw edges of lining opening and press. Sew opening closed by machine or hand. Push lining into tote.

5. Press along tote's top edge and topstitch. Sew additional row of topstitching ¼" [.75 cm] below previous topstitching.

Load your tote with your must-have essentials and you're finished!

Anna is the owner of Noodlehead sewing patterns and is based in Wisconsin.
www.noodle-head.com Instagram: noodlehead531

Scales Wallhanging
by Carolyn Friedlander

Scales Wallhanging Quilt
by Carolyn Friedlander

Inspired by both the life of water and the living things beneath the surface, my Scales project is a fun way to explore creating texture and life, both in the piecing and at the surface.

Finished Size
17½" [44.5 cm] tall x 20" [51 cm] wide

Supplies
- About ¾ yard [68.5] total in assorted blue fabrics
- ¼ yard [22.75 cm] binding fabric
- ⅝ yard [57.25 cm] backing fabric
- 22" x 24" [56 cm x 61 cm] batting
- Embroidery floss
- Embroidery needle
- Removable marking tool

Notes
All seam allowances are ¼" [.75 cm].

I created a textured tapestry of water for my background with both thick, thin, long and short sections in a range of deep blues. Simply cut the strips and strip sections to create a mix of sections large and small. Use a design wall and take a step back to see how sections are working as a whole. I wanted to create more intensity where I would be embroidering the fish, and so I incorporated smaller strip sections in that area.

Wallhanging
1. Cut and position assorted blue fabrics into strips as shown in Diagram 1 and as listed in Row Chart (next page), piecing together multiple sections as desired so that strip length is at least 21" [53.25 cm].

Row Chart

Row	Strip Size	Row	Strip Size
1	1¾" [4.5 cm]	10	¾" [2 cm]
2	1" [2.5 cm]	11	1" [2.5 cm]
3	2½" [6.25 cm]	12	1" [2.5 cm]
4	1½" [3.75 cm]	13	1½" [3.75 cm]
5	1¼" [3.25 cm]	14	1¼" [3.25 cm]
6	1½" [3.75 cm]	15	1¼" [3.25 cm]
7	1" [2.5 cm]	16	1½" [3.75 cm]
8	¾" [2 cm]	17	1¼" [3.25 cm]
9	2½" [6.25 cm]	18	3" [7.5 cm]

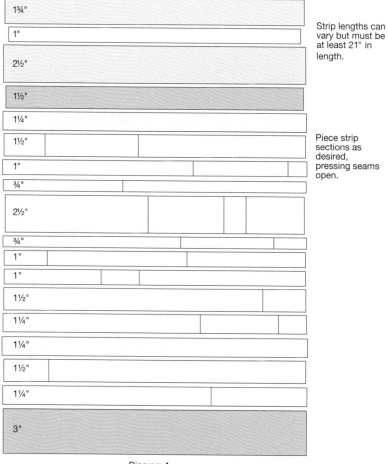

Strip lengths can vary but must be at least 21" in length.

Piece strip sections as desired, pressing seams open.

Diagram 1

Note: Join strip sections first, press seams open.

2. Attach rows together, pressing each seam open.

Tip: Some rows are very narrow. Pin carefully and press open after each seam.

3. Square piece and trim to 17½" [44.5 cm] tall and 20" [51 cm] wide. See Diagram 2.

4. Position and mark fish (see Fish drawings at right) with removable marking tool, or freehand fish as desired.

5. With 2 strands of embroidery floss, follow fish markings using the back stitch.

6. Once embroidery is complete, layer backing (right side down), batting and embroidered top (right side up). Baste layers together and quilt as desired.

7. Trim excess batting and backing. Bind project.

Carolyn is a quilter and the author of Savor Each Stitch. *She is based in Florida.*
www.carolynfriedlander.com
Instagram: carolynfriedlander

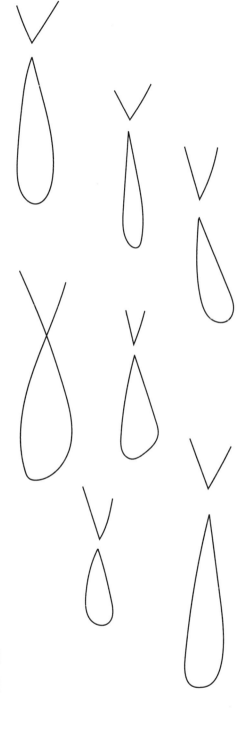

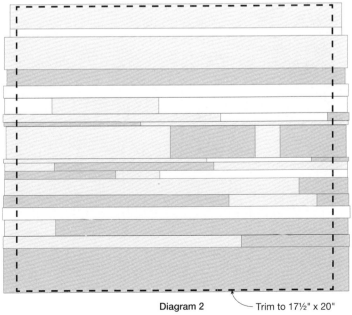

Diagram 2   ⌐ Trim to 17½" x 20"

HANDSPUN

Handspun by Ashley Yousling

Camellia Fiber Co. yarn

knit pattern on pgs 102–103

Orchard Grass Stole
by Ashley Yousling

Knitted with Ashley's own handspun yarn

Camellia Tank
by Karen Templer

Knitted with Camellia Fiber Co. handspun yarn

knit pattern on pgs 104–106

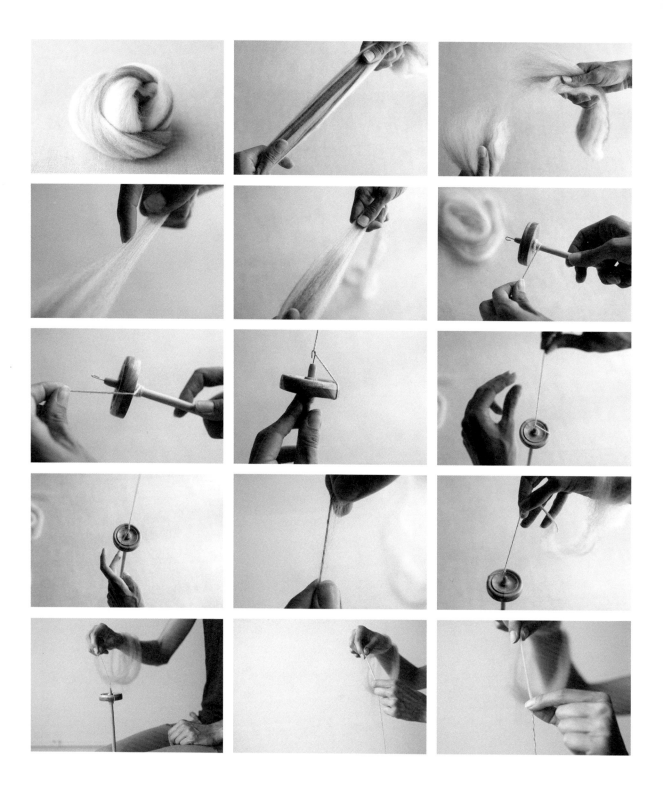

Drop Spindle Spinning Tutorial
by Casey Ryder

I love the simplicity of a drop spindle and its connection to our past as makers. It's portable, efficient, and gives us yet another opportunity to touch wool!

Supplies
- Wool top or roving
- Top or bottom whorl spindle, approx 1–1½ oz [28.5–42.5 grams]

Notes about Wool
You will want to start your spindle spinning journey with a wool fiber that has a 3–4" [8–10.5 cm] staple length. Plant fibers can often be a tricky length (too short or too long) and other protein/animal fibers can be too slippery (alpaca, silk). Wool fibers will have a delightful grabby factor because of their crimp structure, and a 3-4" [8–10.5 cm] staple length is the sweet spot when you're learning. Determine the staple length by pulling off a couple of hairs and seeing how long they are. Top is fiber that has been combed is known as a worsted prep. When you spin top, you'll get a smoother yarn because the fibers are running parallel to one another and are generally the same length. Roving is fiber that has been carded and is known as a woolen prep. When you spin roving, you'll get a yarn that is fluffier and traps more air because the fibers are a bit more jumbled and are often a variety of lengths. Woolen yarns tend to be warmer, fuzzier, and less shiny than worsted yarn.

Notes about Spindles
Spindles come in all shapes and sizes, made from a variety of lovely materials. Look for a spindle that appeals to your senses, of course! You want to be making beautiful yarn with a beautiful tool. But also look for a spindle between 1–1½ oz [28.5-42.5 grams]. This is a mid-weight spindle. Lighter spindles are better for lacier yarns. Heavier spindles are better for heavier yarns.

Some spindles are weighted on the top, others on the bottom. Both work in the same manner. Support spindles, however, are a different beast. We're just sticking with good ol' bottom or top weighted spindles for now.

To Spin
1. Pre-draft your wool. Pre-drafting is thinning out your wool before you spin it. You will draft as you spin too, but pre-drafting gets your hands used to the fiber. To pre-draft, pull off a foot of your top or roving by holding your hands further apart than the staple length. If your hands are gripping within the staple length of the wool, then you are pulling on the same fibers and they will not slide past one another. This is important. When you pre-draft, your hands must be further apart than the staple length. Working with that foot of top or roving, grip the wispy bits of fiber with one hand and grasp the rest of the fiber with your other hand at a distance a tad longer than the staple length. Gently pull the wispy bits and watch where the fibers start sliding past one another. That is where you're going to grab next. This is often referred to as the "drafting triangle." Where the fibers are sliding past one another is the tip of the next triangle. The base is where you are securing the fibers with your other hand.

If you grab too far into your fiber supply, you will end up with a lump. The key is to focus between your hands on where those fibers are sliding apart and make your next grab in that spot.

As you draft, you will move the hand securing your fibers back to allow more fiber forward. Try to grip all of the fibers with an even amount of pressure as you pre-draft.

2. Attach the fiber to your spindle. Use a piece of waste yarn and secure it to your spindle shaft near the whorl. Wind the waste yarn onto the shaft and then run it through the groove in the whorl and through the hook if it's a top whorl. If it is a bottom whorl and doesn't have a hook, make a half hitch at the end of the shaft.

Draft out a few wisps from your pre-drafted fiber and overlap these with your leader yarn about 4 or 5" [10.5–13 cm]. Pinch the tips of the wisps with the hand that you were drafting with. Spin the spindle clockwise with the hand that was securing the fibers—I use my thumb and middle finger. This will build up twist in the leader yarn. Do this a few times, keeping your pinch tight with your drafting hand.

3. Park and draft. Set your spindle down on a table or hold it between your knees. Move the hand that was spinning the spindle to where your other hand was and pinch in the same spot. Now draft a few fibers out and slide your pinch into those drafted fibers. Remember the drafting triangle, and focus on the space between your hands. Continue in this manner—draft, slide—for maybe 6-8" [15.5–20 cm]. Depending on how much twist you've built up, you may need to draft less or more. Fiber needs twist to hold together. If you draft too much length, your new yarn will fall apart.

If you are finding it hard to draft, one problem may be that your hands are too close to one another and you are gripping the same staple. Another problem may be that there is a slight amount of twist between your hands. If the twist gets beyond your pinch hand, sneaking into your drafting zone, it can make it difficult to draft.

After drafting out a length that is 6-10" [15.5–25.5 cm], switch your pinch hand again, and give your spindle another few clockwise flicks. Set your spindle down and draft out some more length. Eventually, you will get a length of yarn that is too long to deal with. Time to wind on!

4. Wind on. Keeping your new yarn under tension, wrap it up around one of your hands. I like to make a figure eight between my thumb and pinky, but any old way will do. Continuing to keep your yarn under tension, turn your spindle and allow the yarn to wind onto the shaft, close to the whorl to start. If you have a Turkish-style spindle, you'll wind on around the "legs."

Make sure to leave enough to attach it to your hook with a few inches to spare before beginning another round of park & draft.

5. Continue to park and draft until drafting feels comfortable. Once you get a feel for drafting, and it does take time, you will be able to spin your spindle and then draft while the spindle is spinning.

Don't jump too quickly to this step, though. It can be daunting. Give your body a chance at some muscle memory. Once you do get to this step, you can stand and spin a longer length before having to wind on.

6. Unwind—ball up your singles. Once you fill up your spindle, wind it off into a ball. If you have a Turkish spindle you have the added benefit of finishing with a center-pull ball. Simply push the legs off the shaft, pull out the legs from the yarn, find your leader yarn, and voila!

Now go on with your bad self and make another singles. Ball that one up, too.

7. Ply! To ply, put each of your singles in a bowl. Hold the ends together and overlap with the leader yarn. Now you are going to spin counterclockwise and no drafting is necessary. Simply allow the two singles to spin together. The goal is to put the same amount of twist in your plied yarn as you did in your singles to balance out the twist!

8. Skein, soak, and dry. Using a niddy noddy or just your arm, wind your yarn into a skein and tie it off in a few places. Give it a soak in some lukewarm water, gently squeezing out the air bubbles. Let it sit for 10–15 minutes. Gently squeeze out excess water, roll it in a towel if you'd like, and hang it to dry. When you hold up your finished skein, if it spins up on itself clockwise, there was a bit more ply twist than singles twist. If it spins up on itself counter clockwise, there was a bit more singles twist than ply twist. If it doesn't twist up on itself it's balanced! Hoorah!

9. Pat yourself on the back—you made your own yarn!

Casey is a fiber-lover based in Portland, ME and the owner of PortFiber.
www.portfiber.com. Instagram: portfiber

HOME

Brandy Milk Punch
by Trey Hughes

Now that the days are getting shorter and there's a chill in the air it's a good time to start dusting off the cold weather drinks. Brandy Milk Punch is often associated with the warmer clime of New Orleans where it is enjoyed year round (frequently as a morning beverage—one of the many things I love about that city!). With the holidays on the horizon, who doesn't need a little extra fortification at the beginning of the day? Of course, you can drink it whenever you like. There's also ample room for adjustments and substitutions. Out of heavy cream? Not to worry. Bump up the milk. Or throw in some half and half. I often split the brandy with dark rum but I hear bourbon works well too.

Brandy Milk Punch

- 1½ oz brandy
- ½ oz whole milk
- ¾ oz heavy cream
- ½ oz 2:1 simple syrup*
- ¼ tsp vanilla extract
- grated nutmeg for garnish

Shake all ingredients with ice. Strain over fresh ice into a rocks glass.
Garnish.

*Combine 2 parts sugar with 1 part hot water and stir to dissolve.

Trey is the bar manager at The Portland Hunt & Alpine Club in Portland, ME.
www.huntandalpineclub.com Instagram: huntandalpine

Caramelized Fig Pear-Ginger Pie
by Tammy White of Wing & A Prayer Farm

Pies are as symbolic of family to me as anything could be. The presence of a pie on my countertop is a souvenir of my childhood, transporting me back to that twelve year old with my grandmother, my hometown's reputed pie baker, tying on my apron. Grandma Brown, calm and quiet: "I will show you how, Tammy, not just tell you. You must make the pie with me." The recipe she used for her pie crusts was her own.

It was a mile long walk from the school bus stop to home, through the meadow where I'd watch goldfinches flit and hawks circle lazily overhead, and hear blue jays squall at each other from high up in the spruce branches. Wild animal life was as contented and ordinary as my own. As normal and natural as my grandmother and I rolling out pie dough together.

In the current day and age, things are a little different, but by no means alienated from my upbringing. In my backyard a young rooster is practicing his crowing and a baby donkey is fiddling with the latch of his paddock gate. I hear sheep bells tinkling out in the far pasture and one of our turkeys is peering over the top of the back step, studying me with curious eyes as I write.

Atop our barn is a weathervane: a peace dove with an olive branch in its beak. The symbolism is often at odds with the mayhem of running a farm—albeit rewarding, enjoyable mayhem. But there is peace, too, in the pattern of the day: sheep chew their cud, chickens lay their eggs, the barn cat stretches out in a sunny spot. Things are balanced this way, balanced as life ever can be. In their own way, tranquility and chaos are as simple as a child's world is. It's as simple and easy as adding a dash of this and a pinch of that and knowing it will be right if the ingredients are fresh and the intention is good. As easy as pie.

Caramelized Fig Pear-Ginger Pie Recipe
by Tammy White of Wing & A Prayer Farm

Pie crust *(Makes one double crusted pie, per recipe I use from my Grandma Brown.)*
- 1⅔ cups flour
- 1 tsp sugar
- ⅛ tsp salt
- 5 tbsp butter
- 1 tsp apple cider vinegar
- ¼ cup ice cold water
- 1 whole egg, whisked well but *only using* 2 tbsp for recipe

Combine dry ingredients and cut in butter with pastry blender or two knives, scissor fashion, until mixture is fine and crumbly. Do not overmix. Whisk together wet ingredients (including partial amount of whisked egg, not entire egg) and add to flour/butter mixture, incorporating a bit at a time until dough comes together in a ball. Add more ice water, a tablespoon at a time, if necessary. Do not overmix.
Cover/wrap dough tightly to prevent drying of edges and refrigerate until 15 minutes before rolling out. Dough can be refrigerated for a day ahead of time, or wrapped and frozen for up to a month.

Prepare caramelized figs
- 1 pint fresh figs (or 1 heaping cup dried figs), washed and sliced in half, stem to stern
- ¼ cup salted butter
- ⅛ cup maple syrup

In cast iron skillet, melt butter to browning over me-dium heat. Add figs and sauté for 5 minutes until heated through and beginning to soften. Drizzle maple syrup over all and allow to cook, uncov-ered and undisturbed, for 5 minutes. Maple syrup should begin to thicken and all ingredients will begin to brown. Carefully move ingredients around to allow sticky, buttery syrup to cover all parts of the figs and turn off heat. Let figs cool in pan.

Prepare ginger-pear filling
- 4 cups of fresh or frozen sliced, peeled pears
- ⅔ cup sugar
- ¼–⅜ cup non-GMO cornstarch
- 2-3 tsp fresh grated ginger, or 1 tsp powdered (amount used depends on your preference)
- 1 tsp ground cinnamon

For assembly and topping
- ⅛ cup of milk for attaching leaf-edging
- 1 egg white, beaten to froth for brushing atop pie
- Coarse crystallized sugar to decorate
- Aluminum foil
- Parchment paper

Whisk together sugar, cornstarch, and cinnamon and combine with pears and fresh ginger.

Prepare decorative crust and assemble
Preheat oven to 350°, line a shallow-edged pan with parchment to place under pie while baking. Remove pie crust from refrigeration, divide in two pieces.

Sprinkle surface with flour for rolling out. Roll pie crust to fill pie pan with a minimal overhang. Pour pear filling into crust, leaving approximately ¾" [2 cm] to top of pan for caramelized figs. Using spatula or your fingers, place figs in a concentric circular pattern, starting from outside, working inward, covering pears.

Keeping surface lightly floured, roll out second disc of crust to top pie. A small leaf-shaped cookie cutter, generously floured, is useful for cutting out a decorative edging for pie. Cut leaf-shaped crust 4 or 5 at a time and brush underside with milk, then press lightly onto outside edge or pie crust. Con-tinue until pie is circled with leaves.

Brush circle of leaves with beaten egg white and sprinkle with coarse sugar. Using strips of alumi-num foil, cover, lightly, outside edge of pie for most of baking time. Do not press the foil into the egg-brushed dough; it may stick when you are remov-ing it and accidentally remove some of the crust.

Bake pie on lined pan in a preheated 350° oven for 45 minutes –1 hour. Remove foil covering in last 10–15 minutes of baking, making sure it does not overbrown.

Making sure remaining crust is workable and easily removed from counter, use a sharp utility knife or kitchen knife, and cut desired decorative topping, such as leaves, stems, and doves, into the remaining dough. A pattern can be made ahead of time and used as a template for design. See page 146 if you would like to copy the bird template provided onto parchment paper. Re-roll pieces if necessary to garner enough surface for pattern. Remove crust decoration with a spatula and gently place on parchment lined baking sheet to bake separately from pie. Remove any residual flour and smooth any ragged edges.

Brush top with egg white and sprinkle with coarse sugar.

Bake for 10–15 minutes in 350° oven. Let cool before placing decorative crust atop baked pie.

Tip: Keep an eye on the browning edges of the pie after removing foil covering to make sure it does not over cook. Also, keep an eye on decorative crust on separate baking sheet while it bakes to make sure it is a similar brown to the pie edging for a uniform look.

See page 152 for helpful links.

Tammy is the owner of Wing and A Prayer Farm and the local pie lady of Shaftsbury, VT.
www.wingandaprayerfarm.com
Instagram: wingandaprayerfarm

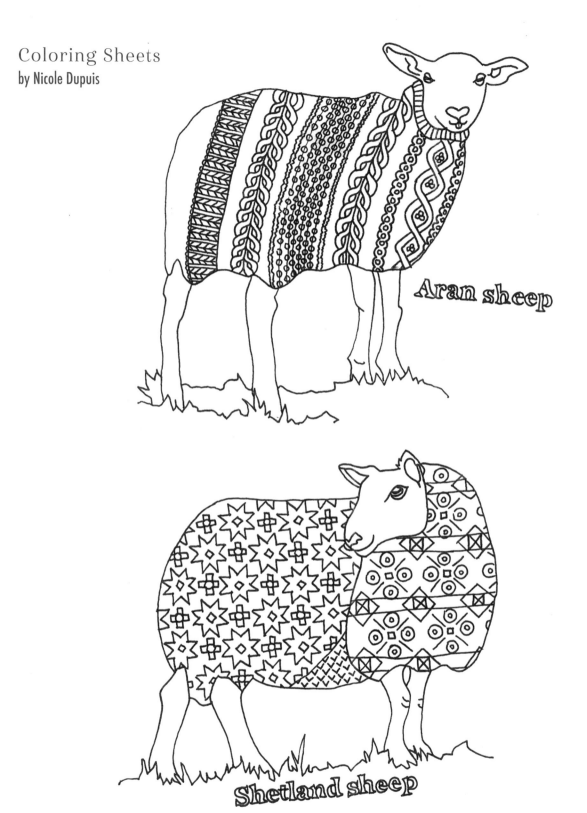

Aran sheep

Shetland sheep

Icelandic sheep

Faroese sheep

Nicole is a knitter and podcaster in Canada.
Instagram: the gentleknitter

HOMESTEAD

East / Amanda Blake Soule

West / Ashley Yousling

A Conversation between Homesteaders

by Amanda Blake Soule and Ashley Yousling

Amanda: I'm writing to you this summer morning, having just come in from morning chores here on our small homestead in Western Maine. Here, we currently have a few pigs, over a hundred chickens (we raise them for meat as well as eggs), some ducks, a small flock of 11 Shetland sheep, and a few Nigerian Dwarf goats. Add a Great Pyrenees, and the obligatory farm cats, plus five children aged 5–15... and well, it's a menagerie out there on our humble 30-acre homestead! Though it hasn't been all that long (we've been on the farm for just six years now), sometimes it all feels so second nature—this rhythm to our days anchored around chores and the cycle of the seasons, that I forget the long journey that it took for us to get to this place. We (my husband Steve and I), spent many years looking for the land and house that we would eventually call home, and even more years working to get to the place where we could combine work and family into one place (home!), which was such an important part of our vision from the beginning. But I'm getting ahead of myself. I know that you, too, are in the midst of a similar such journey for your family. Can you tell us a little about that? Where you're coming from, where you'd like to be and where you are in that process now?

Ashley: At the moment I happen to be sitting upstairs in my local cafe, a comely place I frequent once or twice a week in an effort to get the majority of my computer work done, for both Woolful and the company I work for in San Francisco. I enjoy working from home the most, though, on our 40 acre ranch nestled between the Selkirk and Cabinet mountains in North Idaho. It's a burgeoning ecosystem, home to our growing herd of 5 Dexter cattle, 12 Icelandic sheep, 6 alpacas, several Red Wattle x Large Black hogs, a myriad of Muscovy ducks, meat and layer chickens, barn cats and of course the heroes of our farm, Fritz, Ernst and Bertie, our Maremma sheepdogs. We're at the very beginning of our journey, having bought the ranch in 2014, which we share with my parents who live in the cabin on the property. Our life has taken a near 180 degree turn these past couple of years and this past summer my husband David and I and our son Coltrane made the move from city life in San Francisco, to making our forever home here in Idaho. It was and is very much a leap of faith for us. A decision that we didn't anticipate

making for some time, preferring to trade our dreams in for the comforts and security of our urban life. But something was pulling us, beckoning us to make some changes and so we did. We bought and built a yurt, and are taking each day as it comes, with its endless list of priorities and its constant 'keep-you-on-your-toes' nature. Much like you, we have a vision for this place, one that is constantly evolving, but began with a single desire...to build a legacy for our children. That desire of course is brimful of intentions...but first, I'd love to hear a bit more about where your journey to homesteading began...your vision and intentions...

Amanda: Our overarching vision and goal for this homestead of ours was to bring all the spheres of our lives into one realm, back to home. Home being the place in the world that we all live, love, work and learn in and around. We wanted our children—and ourselves—to truly know a place. To know not just the street we may live on but the trees and the rocks of the woods, or to feel deep in their bones the changing of the season by noticing the way the stream at the back of our property rises and falls as the months change. I wanted there to be ample space for all of us to wander, daydream, and 'get lost' in the woods. One can never be bored with space like that, can we? Our hope was that this homestead would provide room for that to happen, as well as offer us enough space to work from home and homeschool too. As well, to have enough room for experimenting with what livestock we wanted to share the land with.

When we moved here, it felt a bit like a blank slate, as despite being a 200 year-old farmhouse, the land had not been farmed for decades. Though at times it certainly would have been easier if something had been done before we got here—say, some fencing! or even rock clearing!—I'm still grateful for the opportunity that we had to create just exactly what we wanted and what would work for us. That process was so enriching for our family as we learned by trial and error, but worked together to make each little dream happen, with a lot of excitement along the way at the newness of it all. For those first six years, so much energy and effort was put into creating spaces and learning how to do the things we

Amanda is a blogger, author, and the editor of Taproot Magazine, a quarterly about food, farm, family and craft. She lives with her husband and five children in an old farmhouse and homestead in Western Maine, where they strive to live closely to the earth and to each other. www.soulemama.com Instagram: soulemama

east / amanda

*Ashley is a knitwear designer and creator of Woolful,
living on her ranch in North Idaho with her growing
family and farm. She's been a maker since childhood,
creating things she found interesting and beautiful,
and sharing them with the world in hopes they would
find them valuable as well.
www.woolful.com Instagram: woolful*

wanted to do. Everything from the arrival of the first meat birds of the year to shearing the sheep or birthing lambs required building something we didn't have, or learning a new skill. And sometimes, we poured energy into things that in the end, didn't end up feeling right for us but we had to walk through to learn that (I'm thinking of dairy cows in particular right here!). We were nurturing and loving this land, the animals and this home with all of our beings, I'd say. And now, I feel like we are in a little bit of a pause, or a transition, where the land and this home is now nurturing us for a little while. No longer are we reinventing the wheel every season for every task. Now, some things are beginning to be second nature, and a rhythm that we can anticipate with comfort and a little more ease. It isn't exactly as though we are working on autopilot, as there is still so much physical work to be done each and every day, but it does come now with a more comfortable and expected rhythm. And that, beautifully, is coming at a time where the demands of our growing children are pulling our energy elsewhere. And so we find ourselves leaving home more often than ever before as the kids grow and stretch and reach outside of home and family to the wider world around them. It's an exciting time for them, for us all really, as that happens. To watch as they go out into the world, and then retreat back home - into the comfort of our home, the friendship of our animals, and the beauty of the woods. I envision the next stretch of years for us looking like this—holding fairly steady on the farm life, maintaining what we have and love here, and letting it love us back!

Ashley: I look forward to a cadence developing. Right now each task seems imperative yet our days are getting shorter, both figuratively and literally as Fall and the birth of our second son approaches. The changing of the seasons also marks a new chapter in our lives, as I prepare to leave the career I've spent the past 10 years building and growing in, to transition into a new season of motherhood and personal ambition—focusing on building and growing our family and farm. I sort of chuckle as I say that, because a short 3 years ago we imagined something very different for our lives. But I guess that's part of what happens when you start a family. Children can have a huge impact on how you see yourself, your values and your future. At least that's what happened to us, and it radically changed our path.

When we moved to the ranch at the end of last summer, our dreams were grand and they fueled us through that first fall as we shared the cabin with my parents while we built our yurt. What we thought would be a straight-forward project turned into a monumental one and it brought us into winter when we finally moved our bed and whittled-down belongings into this off-grid, round abode. We fell in love that winter—with our land, with our growing farm and more with each other. I watched in amazement as dreams became real, and new dreams took hold. This was a form of creative expression I had yet to experience, building something we could call our own—building a home and a legacy. While the winter was considered a shorter one, the frigid temperatures taught us much about ourselves and began to shape what our next year would look like. The first being the understanding that much work must be done when the ground is soft and dry. This meant that all the insulating, trenching, building, and growing would need to be done in a meager 4 months. In spite of all the well intentioned plans, you're not in control and flexibility is key. Or as my good ranching friend Mary always tells me, "Wax your board and ride the wave. You'll have a lot more fun." This means things have changed from our initial short and long term vision. Our garden is a fraction of what we'd planned, the yurt has a lot of work to be done yet, there's a barn that needs building, pastures to be fenced and so on. It's not where we thought we'd be at the end of this season, but it's exactly where we want to be.

But when we close our eyes, this is what we see. A full wood shed brimming with pride as it welcomes the fall which brings us glorious yellows in the form of Tamaracks, Cottonwoods, Birch, and Aspen trees. Smoke rising out of the chimney of our stone home, built on the hill with our own hands, with stones from our land, and warming our growing family. Snow falling and beckoning us to strap on our cross country skis and explore, eventually making our way around the farm to resupply hay and water for our animals that provide a kind of benevolence only they can, in the form of food on our table and wool on our backs, beds and floors. And with the spring thaw, life takes on a whole new meaning…our beehives are full of energy just waiting for those wild flowers and cover crops to bloom, our children watching in amazement at

the spectacle these hives are. The steam is beginning to rise in the repurposed wood and windowed 100-foot-long greenhouse, seedlings making their way up as they're protected from our late frosts. The expansive barn built from the timber that surrounds us and milled on the very ground it sits on, is burgeoning with new life as well… singles, twins, triplet lambs, maybe a foal from our draft horse crosses or a cria or two. Our now much larger herd of Dexter cattle calving in the pasture, udders full for their new babes—and us anxiously anticipating filling our small creamery with fresh cheese, milk, and butter—and replenishing the troughs of our heritage hogs and their piglets. These calves, piglets and lambs will eventually find their way to new homes, to provide for families just like they have for us, whether it be as breeding stock, for food or fiber. With life so abundant on the farm, we find ourselves at our local farmers' market, sharing a bit of all of this with our community. Summer is the season of harvest, putting up and preparing for the fall. We hay half our land in hopes that it'll get us through the winter, giving our rotated pastures a much needed break while they rest under the snow. When we close our eyes, this is what we see.

Amanda: Oh, that's a beautiful vision! And your friend Mary is really onto something with her advice —"Wax your board and ride the wave. You'll have a lot more fun." So true! We never do know exactly what the wave will hold, do we? When I look back at the goals we first set all those years ago, and see what we have around us now, there are certainly so many aspects that are not what we had envisioned. Things we let go of, things that we are still years away from. But the important things remain and are a fundamental part of our days. I had always anticipated the relationship that my children would have with the animals we share our time with, and that's certainly come to fruition tenfold. There is so much to learn from

watching the life cycle on a farm, and embracing all that comes with it—the joy of birth and the sadness of death. We have seen all of that, and walked through it together as a family. Such hard lessons, but so honestly and deeply felt when you live alongside animals in this way. And then there is the companionship, joy, entertainment and peace to be found by their daily company! Whenever there are moments of doubt that we have about whether or not we are on the right path, or whether all this work is actually worth it…I will inevitably find one of my children way back in the pasture singing a song for a baby lamb, or tending a hurt chicken, or running to see the goats to ease her anxiety about something. I know with certainty that our family will for the rest of our days remember our favorite duck who lives with the chickens and thinks she is one, and I know that we will likely talk about that time we needed to help with a particularly difficult goat birth, with a newly-reading child at my side, trying her best to instruct from the farm manual, five year old sister narrating the entire process, and brother shining his flashlight so that we could see! These are the stories that connect us, and the ties that bind our family together. These animals we share our land with—and yes, even the ones we eventually feed our bodies with—are such a gift to us, and such a help to me in mothering my children for all of those reasons.

Ashley: You said it perfectly. We've been told many times that the first lesson in farming is 'life and death' and that's held true for us as well and there's a richness in these raw experiences, making your own existence much more precious. Whether I'm putting a maimed layer chicken to rest with a curious yet sensitive toddler by my side or standing in the pasture at 2:30am in after-birth stained pajamas, gathering a fresh calf in David's coat and helping him bond to his mama. Or the three of us standing in the stable, mourning the loss of a drowned lamb as we

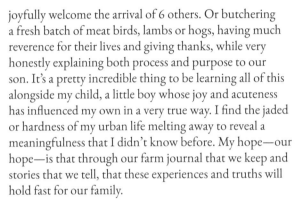

joyfully welcome the arrival of 6 others. Or butchering a fresh batch of meat birds, lambs or hogs, having much reverence for their lives and giving thanks, while very honestly explaining both process and purpose to our son. It's a pretty incredible thing to be learning all of this alongside my child, a little boy whose joy and acuteness has influenced my own in a very true way. I find the jaded or hardness of my urban life melting away to reveal a meaningfulness that I didn't know before. My hope—our hope—is that through our farm journal that we keep and stories that we tell, that these experiences and truths will hold fast for our family.

Amanda: Yes, that experience will be his truth, and the lessons our children are learning now will stay with them forever. I do not have any false hope or assumptions that any of our children will carry on with this homestead, though of course we'd welcome that and be pleased. Right now, ironically, their visions and dreams (at least the oldest ones who are closer to thinking about such things) are of urban areas and metropolitan living. Wonderful! But I do hope that wherever they go, they carry with them this farm and all they've learned here—about land, about animals and food, and about themselves. About the responsibility we have to all that is around us. And I hope they learn to think a little bit deeper about where things come from, and how they were made. Being involved in a natural process from beginning to end is such a gift in not only skill but in gratitude and patience too. And these things they are learning not only from the animals we care for and the garden we tend, but also in the things we make. Making things is so deeply entrenched in our daily lives here—from the elderberries I harvested this morning to make cough syrup to last through the winter, to the tomatoes in my oven right now headed soon to the

canner for soups and stews in the coming months, and of course, to the yarn always in my hands. That's been one of the greatest personal joys for me in all of this. I have loved knitting for so long, and thought I loved sheep too, but what did I know, really? Nothing! Ha! But it turns out, thank goodness, that I do. I LOVE our sheep (there is no level of stress that sitting with the sheep for twenty minutes can't ease). And then between that place of tending sheep and knitting garments, I've slowly learned and filled the gaps of knowledge over recent years. From learning how to shear. Then learning how to spin. And now, experimenting with so many natural dyes on the finished fiber. I have loved every step of that process that brings me (and my children too!) so much joy. I know that this particular kind of making is a big part of your own motivation to farm, yes?

Ashley: Our dream of owning land and building a farm really all began with making. My keen interest in knitting grew into an obsession with fiber which introduced me to a whole new world. I had a desire to know where things come from and who's responsible for growing/creating these things and my own responsibility in all of that. We began spending our weekends on farm and ranches, meeting the folks responsible and finding ourselves with rapidly growing dreams and knowledge, that first lamb camp workshop we attended, the small livestock butchering clinic, a lesson in shearing from our neighbor, a course in master beekeeping. What began as dreams of having our own fiber flock, bled into full fledged farm reality. And yet each day I find myself tending to that very first image …whether I'm shearing, sorting or spinning my sheep's fleece, knitting a jumper for our new babe, or producing a Woolful podcast. All of this is a part of the very dear thing we all call making.

EXPLORE

Nash Island Sheep Shearing
Essay by Mary Jane Mucklestone

Nash is an island in Maine inhabited only by sheep. Sheep and gulls. Once upon a time, a hundred years ago, a family lived in a lighthouse on the next tiny island, and the lighthouse keeper's daughter, Jenny, kept a flock of sheep. The descendants of these sheep still live on these islands, all by themselves, with the gulls. The islands lie in the middle of the blue of the sea and the blue of the sky. They are nearly flat, with no trees, only brambles, short grasses and bog. Stony grey beach surrounds them, strewn with seaweed and bleached driftwood.

It's a magical place.

Every year, this community of sheep is invaded by another community. A small flotilla of lobster boats arrive with a lively crew of humans set for shearing the flock's lovely fog washed fleece. They've been doing it for years, the same group of people: family, old friends, and a smattering of new friends. As people wade ashore, unloading the boats by passing needed supplies hand to hand, the sheep take one look and head for the far side of the island—having none of it.

Coffee and breakfast breads lure the folk together so Alfie Wakeman can explain the drill. As a child he summered nearby and became close friends with Jenny Cirone, the shepherdess. She taught him how to fish for lobster and they fished and tended her sheep together until she died at 91. Jenny gave the islands and sheep over to Alfie and he and his family have been the stewards ever since, doing things the way Jenny always did them.

Rounding up the sheep is done without dogs, only people. Alfie explains the time tested strategy. A couple of runners, head out to circle the edge of the island, herding the sheep along the coast, while separate teams of people hide in clumps in the bog and field, trying their best to look like rocks. As the sheep pass them, these teams stand up and stretch their arms wide to discourage the sheep from retreating or heading inland. As more groups stand up, all move forward in wide-armed paper doll lines, encouraging the sheep into the weathered pens by the shore.

Now the real work begins. Separating the lambs from their mothers, "lamb tossing," is a lively and challenging operation. Fearless teenagers grab lambs from amidst the mass of wooly baaing ewes and hand them over the fence where they are passed off to someone else who carries the flailing lamb—all pink ears and sharp little hooves—over to another person situated in the lamb pen. Here they are checked and administered to and set free.

The mothers are not happy with this situation. Their crying and calling out to their babies will continue all day.

The shearing itself is spectacular. Four amazing women on the mats, shears sharpened. Donna Kausen and Geri Valentine have each been shearing for 35+ years, while Eleni, Alfie's wife, has been at it for 8, and 2016 was their eldest daughter Wren's second. Their strength, stamina and precision is astounding. The sheep are wrangled one by one out of the pens and on to the mats, grabbed by the shearer and together with the wrangler put on their rumps, and clamped between the shearer's legs. Working along side the shearer are the fleece tenders, who pick off the worst of the soiled fleece and belly wool, and as it is being shorn, 'roll' the fleece in a special way to ensure that its stays intact and opens tip side up. Fleece tenders must be nimble, act quickly and not get in the way of the shearers or wranglers. In between shearing the sweeper keeps the mats clean with a quick pass of the broom.

The newly shorn fleeces are handed over to Jani Estell, island wool manager and owner of Starcroft Fiber Mill, a gem—my hero—with a sly smile, sparkly eyes and dry wit, who never seems to hurry yet keeps the whole show going. She has a special touch for sorting fleeces. Fleeces with the longest staple fiber, shiny and lustrous, are reserved for hand spinning (sold before they are even off the

animals). The soft silky first shearing lamb fleece are for her very special Fog yarn. The prime ewe fleece, long and soft with a fine crimp are for Nash Island Light, a luscious worsted weight yarn. Soft bouncy fleece that's "scoodgy" (a made up word because one was lacking) and crimped is for Tide, the dk weight yarn often used for colorwork. No island wool is wasted and anything that does not make the grade is used for felting fiber—reported to be the best out there.

As Jani calls out the grade, the fleeces fly on the skirting table where a small legion of fiber enthusiasts skirt them. Though the island lifestyle keeps the fleeces incredibly clean, there are still odd bits of brambles, seaweed and soiled areas that must be pulled out. The fleeces are carefully rolled up in vintage floral sheets, labeled and later put into huge burlap bags. Jani will hand skirt every fleece a second time when they get to her mill.

When the sun is directly overhead it's time to break for an unbelievable potluck spread. Shearers eat first! After refueling and resting the shearing will continue. When finally finished and the sun approaches the waterline, the whole crowd will load the boats with fleece and gear and head for the mainland happy and satisfied with a job well done. The final task of the day is dropping the rams off on a different smaller island to spend the summer away from the girls, ensuring no lambs will be inconveniently born in winter—and a reason you find so many islands called Ram amongst Maine's coastal islands.

On Nash, the ewes and lambs are relieved to be reunited and happy to have the island to themselves again.

Find Nash Island wool turned into knitting yarn at Starcroft Fiber Mill in Columbia, Maine (starcroft.moon-fruit.com). Each fleece is gently washed in bio-degradable soap. Once dry the fibers are hand-fed into the carding, drafting and spinning machines. The finished yarns are hand-dyed by Jani in small batches with colors inspired by the coastal beauty of Downeast Maine.

Mary Jane is a knitwear designer who likes to share what she knows. She likes to travel, walk through the woods to the top of the hill, and eat popsicles in the summer. www.MaryJaneMucklestone.com Instagram: mjmucklestone

Swatch Diaries
feather inspiration
by Carrie Bostick Hoge

Yarn: Thelma & Louise yarn by Wing & A Prayer farm
(50% Mohair, 25% Cotswold, 25% Merino)
Stitch Exploration from Arctic Cowl, pattern on page 125

Feathers: Betty the Rooster who resides on this farm.

Carrie is a knitter and photographer in Maine.
www.maddermade.com Instagram: maddermade

KIDS

Doe Cap
by Jenny Gordy

knit pattern on pgs 107–108

Squirrel
by Grainline Studio

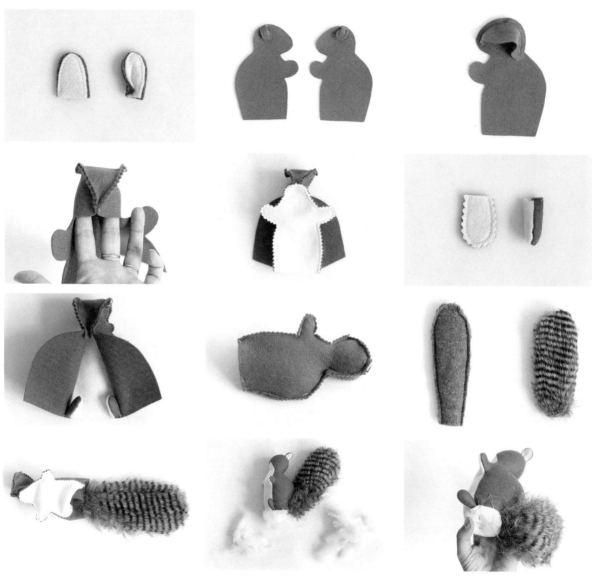

Squirrel
by Grainline Studio

On crisp fall mornings in the Grainline studio, we listen to squirrels outside rustling around in the leaves, gathering seeds and acorns for the winter. They are playful and occasionally jump up on our windowsill to say hello! These squirrels are instant conversation starters. What if they come inside?! We share our stories about squirrels and sometimes even relate to their personalities. We wish we had nuts to feed them. Up here in the north we have a lot in common with the squirrels. We are electric and playful in the summer, keeping ourselves busy knowing that the long summer days are fleeting. As it gets cold, we slow down and prepare for the winter by gathering food for our pantries and quilts for our beds. We collect patterns and projects to keep us busy during the coming winter. We hope this squirrel brings you joy to make as the seasons turn cool.

Supplies
- ¼ yd [22.75 cm] fabric for the main body
- ¼ yd [22.75 cm] contrast fabric for the belly, paws & ears
- ¼ yd [22.75 cm] fabric for the tail
- Fiberfill stuffing
- Thread
- Embroidery floss
- Hand sewing and embroidery needles
- Scissors
- Marking pen or pencil
- Chopstick or bodkin for turning
- Pinking shears (optional)

Recommended fabrics
For main and contrast body: felt, cotton, wool, fleece.
For tail: faux fur or other fuzzy fabric.

Note
All seam allowances are ¼" [.75 cm] unless otherwise noted in the specific step.

Squirrel
1. Cut all pattern pieces (see templates pages 148–149), taking care to transfer all notches and pattern markings.

2. To make the ears, align the inner ears on top of the outer ears with wrong sides together. Stitch around the curved edges using a ⅛" [.5 cm] seam allowance. On the inner ears only, trim the seam allowance in half. Fold the edge of each ear over to meet the center notch and stitch across the bottom at ⅛" [.5 cm] to secure this fold.

3. Pin the ears face down to the body pieces between the notches marked on the top of the head. The folded edge of the ear should fall towards the front of the head, so the ear opening falls to the back. Stitch at ⅛" [.5 cm] to secure the ear to the head.

4. With right sides together, pin head gusset to one body piece. Align one of the short ends of the gusset with the nose notch, the two center gusset notches with the ear notches, then bring the gusset down the back of the head. You'll be stitching from the nose notch to the point marked on the back neck of your body pattern.

5. Next, pin the other side of the body to the gusset aligning the same points as in Step 4. After

sewing both sides of the body to the gusset either clip every ¼" [.75 cm], or trim the seam allowance with pinking shears to encourage smooth curves.

6. Pin the belly to the body with right sides facing each other aligning the notches, matching points, and the bottom edges. Stitch starting at the bottom edge, work your way up around through the face, then back down to the bottom edge on the other side. Clip into the corners at the neck edges and arms, and treat the rest of the seam allowances as you did in Step 5.

7. To make the feet, pin one main foot piece to a contrast foot piece with right sides together. Sew along the curved edge, leaving the bottom of the foot open. Trim the seam allowance with pinking shears or clip around the curve. Repeat for other foot. Flip the feet right side out using your bodkin or chopstick as an aid. Fill feet lightly with stuffing being careful not to overfill. Pinch the opening of the foot closed so that the seam allowances meet. Stitch across the feet at ⅛" [.5 cm] to secure the stuffing inside before attaching them to the body.

8. Pin feet to the body along the hem, between the notches at each side seam. Be sure to match the seam line on the foot and body. Stitch the feet to the body with a ⅛" [.5 cm] seam allowance to secure the feet in place.

9. Pin the center back seam together with right sides facing each other, matching all notches and markings, and making sure that the head gusset seam allowance is out of the way. Sew from the back of the neck down to the hem.

10. Pin the tail pieces together with right sides facing. If you're using a furry fabric be sure to tuck the fur to the inside of the tail so it doesn't get caught in the seams. Flip tail right side out. Coax any fur that has been caught in the seam out with a pin or rattail comb. Stuff the tail very lightly: not so much that the tail becomes full and firm – just enough to give it some volume and life.

11. Pin the bottom of the tail to the center back of the squirrel bottom between the notches. Stitch in place at ⅛" [.5 cm] to secure the tail.

12. Flip the squirrel right side out and begin stuffing. Start with the head and arms and fill until they are firm and hold their shape. Finish stuffing the rest of the squirrel's body until it is full and firm.

13. Align the base over the open bottom of the squirrel and pin in place. Hand stitch around the base, tucking the seam allowance inside as you go.

14. Hand tack the backside of the tail to the top of the squirrel's back hump. Curl the tip of the tail downward and tack the tip of the tail to the back of the tail to create the signature squirrel curl!

15. Using an embroidery needle and floss, create the nose by stitching a small upside down triangle at the nose point. Fill the transferred eye placement with a few embroidery stitches as well. Feel free to get creative with your squirrel's face details.

Your new squirrel friend is now finished and ready for snuggling!

Grainline Studio makes sewing patterns in Chicago, IL. www.grainlinestudio.com Instagram: grainlinestudio

Fox Tooth Fairy Pillow
by Sanae Ishida

The fall theme of Fauna immediately brought to mind a little fox, reminiscent of the gorgeous autumnal reds. Plus, how can you not love a foxy tooth fairy pillow?

Finished Size
4" x 4" [10 cm x 10 cm]

Supplies
• Scraps of very thin linen or cotton (recommended colors: rust and white for the fox, grey for the pillow)
• Marking tool
• Pointy tool for pushing out corners
• Coordinating thread
• Polyfill or cotton batting/stuffing
• Hand-sewing needles
• Sashiko or embroidery thread

Recommended fabrics
Try to use very thin linen or cotton (such as lawn) for the origami shapes to reduce bulk when folding. It's a good idea to prep the fabrics by washing and drying, but it's not entirely necessary for these small pillows. Do make sure to press your fabrics before cutting them out, since you want to start with accurately measured and flat pieces for the origami steps.

Make the fox
1. With the template provided (see page 150), create a pattern piece either by tracing the shape onto another piece of paper or cutting the template out.

2. Trace the shape onto fabric using your preferred marking tool. Cut one piece of fox-colored fabric and one piece of white fabric.

3. With RS facing, stitch around the edge with a ¼" [.75 cm] seam allowance and leave about a 2" [5 cm] opening along the longest straight edge. Clip the corners and turn right side out, pushing out the corners with a point turner. Be careful not to poke holes through the seam. Press, making sure to tuck in the seam allowance at the opening so that it is flush with the rest of the seam.

4. Fold the pointy corner of the triangle towards the long, straight edge.

5. Fold each outer corner back to form the ears. Make sure that part of the white fabric is showing to give the fox face shape.

6. Using coordinating thread, stitch ears to top of head. Don't stitch the entire ear; you'll want to leave an opening of about 1¾" [4.5 cm] for the pocket opening. Then stitch curved edges to the white section of the fox face. (Using white thread works well for the curved edges.)

7. Using black embroidery thread, embroider nose and eyes. For added embellishment, embroider the ears with light-colored thread.

Assemble fox and pillow
1. For the pillow, cut two 4½" x 4½" [11.5 cm x 11.5 cm] squares of fabric.

2. Pin the fox to the center on the RS of one of the squares. It's faster to machine stitch, but I find I have more control when I slip stitch the shape by hand. Sew all around the shape, making sure to leave the pocket opening.

3. If desired, add decorative Sashiko stitches on the pillow fabric.

4. With RS facing, pin and stitch around the pillow with a ¼" [.75 cm] seam allowance, leaving about a 2" [5 cm] opening on the bottom.

5. Clip the corners, turn the pillow RS out, and use a point turner to poke out the corners. Be careful not to poke holes through the seam.

6. Fill the pillow with your choice of stuffing. Slip stitch the opening closed.

7. Let your child roll or fold up his or her note to the tooth fairy and place it, along with the tooth, into the hidden pocket. Let the anticipation begin!

Sanae is the author of Sewing Happiness *and lives in Seattle, WA.*
www.sanaeishida.com Instagram: sanaeishida

Illustrations by Sanae Ishida

opening

opening

Woodland Finger Puppets
by Mollie Johanson

Embroidered Nesting Woodland Puppets
Mollie Johanson

Not too long ago, I would not have considered myself an "animal person." Yes, I've always had pets and sometimes I take care of critters for others while they are traveling, and sure, I may have enjoyed watching the chipmunks in the yard. But I didn't really get excited about animals. That has changed, and I now go a little crazy for the fauna I encounter every day.

Woodland animals are especially lovely to me, and my favorite way to interact with them is by drawing them in the cutest way I possibly can and then embroidering them. To me, capturing them this way is even better than sketching in a nature journal.

With this project, I have gone a step further and made four little animal friends that go from illustrations to embroideries to puppets with which you can truly interact. They can act out a scene together or simply be a friend for your little one to carry around with them. And when they're done playing, they will nest together for easy storage.

Supplies
- ¼ yard [22.75 cm] natural linen fabric
- ½ yard [45.75 cm] fusible mid-weight interfacing
- Water-soluble stabilizer (such as Sulky Sticky Fabri-Solvy)
- Embroidery floss in Black, Brown, Gray, Red-Brown, Tan, and Pink
- Iron
- Scissors
- Pencil
- Embroidery hoop
- Pins
- Sewing machine

Optional: Pinking Shears

Stitches used: Back stitch, French knot, satin stitch, and straight stitch.

Puppets
1. Iron the fusible interfacing to the back of the linen. You will need to piece it a bit, but that's okay. Just be sure to pay attention to where the seam is and avoid placing a pattern over it. Trace two of each of the puppet templates (See page 147) onto the linen with interfacing. Do not trace them too close to the edge of the fabric, or it will make embroidery trickier.

2. Trace or print the animal embroidery patterns (See page 150 for Bear and all others on opposite page) onto the stabilizer and apply them to one set of the template shapes, matching the size of the animal to the size of the template. Embroider the animals with 3 strands of embroidery floss, using back stitch for the outlines, French knots for the eyes, satin stitch for the noses and bear paw, and straight stitch for the fur texture.

3. Soak away the stabilizer, let the embroidery dry, and iron the fabric from the back. Cut out the template shapes, using pinking shears to help prevent fraying, if you like. Press the bottom edge of each puppet piece in about ½" [1.25 cm]. Hand stitch along the hem with running stitch and three strands of coordinating embroidery floss.

4. Match up the pieces and pin them with right sides together and the bottom edges aligned. Sew around the sides and curved edges with a seam allowance of about ⅜" [1 cm]. Backstitch at the beginning and end. Clip the curves and turn the puppets right side out. Press them gently to open the seams and remove wrinkles.

Mollie Johanson has loved creating and crafting cute things for as long as she can remember. She is the author of Stitch Love: Sweet Creatures Big & Small. *Mollie lives near Chicago and is happiest with a cup of coffee, some stitching, and her family close at hand.*
www.molliejohanson.com Instagram: molliejohanson

knit pattern on pg 109-112

77

Narwhals & Friends
by Kim Hamlin

Needle Felt Narwhals
by Kim Hamlin

I adore making miniature animals. There is something so fun about studying a creature and carefully trying to match its exact colors and facial expressions with fiber. I know I'm not alone in this fascination since many a customer has left my shop, arms full of new supplies, after falling in love with one of our sample creatures. It amazes me that wool, a material that comes from an animal on land, can so perfectly capture the texture and color of ocean life. With just a few, easy to make shapes, you can make yourself a pod of narwhals or a handful of other ocean friends.

Materials
• Wool roving, ½ oz [14.5 grams] each in grey, dark grey, white and blue. *Narwhal kits available at www.makingzine.com*
• 38 or 40 Gauge felting needle or, if you prefer, a multi-needle tool
• Wooden skewer or toothpick
• Plastic felting pad or brush

Body
1. Gently loosen the roving and arrange it into a 3" [8 cm] by 10" [25.5 cm] strip.

2. Using your hands, roll fiber into a cylindrical shape.

3. Use shallow stabs of your needle to felt outer layer into place first, then slightly deeper stabs to begin to shape the body. Final shape should look like an elongated egg, with one end slightly bigger and more round than the other. Leave fibers looser at the small end as they will be used to attach the tail fin. You can always add more fiber to make the head the right shape.

Tusk
1. Gently loosen blue roving and arrange it into a 1" [2.5 cm] by 4" [10.5 cm] strip.

2. Fold one end of roving over skewer. Use needle to felt next to skewer in order to hold fibers in place for the next step. *Be careful not to stab the skewer; it can break your needle!*

3. Wrap fibers around the skewer to make a thin cone shape.

4. Roll in your hand to tighten the fiber, shaping one end smaller than the other.

5. Remove skewer and needle felt the end to a tight, pointed shape. Leave fibers loose at wider end.

6. Attach loose fibers of the tusk to the body as shown in photo.

Fins
1. Take a pinch of fiber and felt it into a flat oval shape, about 1" [2.5 cm] in length by ½" [1.25 cm] wide.

2. After about 10 stabs, flip your work over work the other side. Continue flipping until all loose fibers have been incorporated.

3. Attach the fin to the body by stabbing loose fibers left at the small end of the body to the center of the fin. Felt until all loose ends have been incorporated on all sides.

4. Using the same method described in steps 1 and 2, make two smaller fins about ¾" [2 cm] in length by ½" [1.25 cm] wide. One end should be fully felted and round, the other, flat and loose.

5. Attach fins to either side of the body, by felting in loose fibers.

Finishing
Make two pinches of dark grey fiber for eyes and felt into place.

With these supplies you can make at least three creatures: try an orca or a seal as shown in the photo.

Kim is co-owner of Fiber & Vine in Norway, ME. www.fiberandvine.com Instagram: fiberandvine

SEA & SHORE

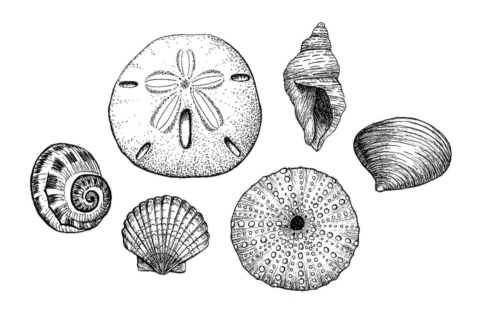

Sea Urchin Treasure Bag
by Mary Jane Mucklestone

knit pattern on pgs 113-114

Byssus Cocoon
by Bristol Ivy

knit pattern on pgs 115–118

Open Waters Shawl
by Melanie Berg

knit pattern on pgs 118–120

knit pattern on pgs 120–121

Open Waters Cowl
by Melanie Berg

knit pattern on pgs 122–124

Arctic Coat & Cowl
by Carrie Bostick Hoge

knit pattern on pg 125

FIELD & FOREST

knit pattern on pgs 125–126

Wild Feather Mitts
by Cecily Glowik MacDonald

Stag Head Pullover
by Norah Gaughan

knit pattern on pgs 127-132

Throstle Shawl
by Bristol Ivy

knit pattern on pgs 132–134

Nyla Hat
by Cal Patch

crochet pattern on pgs 141–143

knit pattern on pgs 135–140

Town-O Cap
by Beatrice Perron Dahlen

knit pattern on pgs 143–144

Orchard Grass Stole
Ashley Yousling

Everything on our farm begins and ends in the soil beneath our feet and the Orchard grass that stretches across our pastures—it feeds our Icelandic sheep that so elegantly grow and provide us with fiber and sustenance. The fiber I used to hand spin the yarn for this design came from my sheep Lucy, a chubby and rambunctious yet lovable ewe. Whether you're a novice or savvy hand spinner, I encourage you to try it—it will enrich your fiber pursuits even more and this stole is the perfectly sized project for such an endeavor.

Finished measurements
15" [38 cm] wide and 48" [122 cm] long
Yarn
Shown in: Handspun single ply wool in lace or light fingering weight
(113 grams / 650 yards [594 meters])
OR
Einband by Ístex
(100% wool; 50 grams / 273 yards [250 meters])
• 3 skeins dark grey 9103
Needles
• One 16" [40 cm] or 24" [60 cm] circular (circ) needle in size US 6 [4 mm]
• One 16" or 24" circ needle in size US 7 [4.5 mm]
Or size to obtain gauge
Notions
• Tapestry needle
Gauge
22 sts and 27 rows = 4" [10 cm] in Orchard Grass pattern with smaller needles, after blocking.
24 sts and 22½ rows = 4" [10 cm] in Old Shale patterns with larger needles, after blocking.

Stitch Patterns
Old Shale Beg (multiple of 18 sts)
(also, see chart)
Row 1: (RS) Knit.
Row 2: Purl.
Row 3: *[K2tog] 3 times, [yo, k1] 6 times, [k2tog] 3 times; rep from * to end.
Row 4: Knit.
Rep Rows 1–4 for Old Shale Beg.

Orchard Grass (multiple of 17 sts)
(also, see chart)
Note: Slip the first stitch of every row purlwise wyib on RS and wyif on WS.
Row 1: (RS) *Sl 1, ssk, k4, yo, k3, yo, k4, k2tog, k1; rep from * to end.
Row 2 and all WS rows: S1, purl to end.
Row 3: Sl 1, ssk, k5, yo, k1, yo, k5, k2tog, k1; rep from * to end.
Row 5: Sl 11, ssk, k3, yo, k5, yo, k3, k2tog, k1; rep from * to end.
Row 7: S1 1, ssk, k4, yo, k3, yo, k4, k2tog, k1; rep from * to end.
Row 9: S1 1, ssk, k2, yo, k7, yo, k2, k2tog, k1; rep from * to end.
Row 11: Sl 1, ssk, k3, yo, k5, yo, k3, k2tog, k1; rep from * to end.
Row 13: Sl 1, ssk, k1, yo, k9, yo, k1, k2tog, k1; rep from * to end.
Row 15: Sl 1, ssk, k2, yo, k7, yo, k2, k2tog, k1; rep from * to end.
Row 17: Sl 1, ssk, yo, k11, yo, k2tog, k1; rep from * to end.
Row 19: Sl 1, ssk, k1, yo, k9, yo, k1, k2tog, k1; rep from * to end.
Row 20: (WS) Sl 1, purl to end.
Rep Rows 1–20 for Orchard Grass.

Old Shale End (multiple of 18 sts)
(also, see chart)
Row 1: (WS) Knit.
Row 2: (RS) *[K2tog] 3 times, [yo, k1] 6 times, [k2tog] 3 times; rep from * to end.
Row 3: Purl.
Row 4: Knit.
Rep rows 1–4 for Old Shale End.

Notes
Circular needles are used to accommodate the large number of sts. Do not join; work back and forth in rows.

When working the Orchard Grass pattern, slip the first stitch of every row purlwise wyib on RS and wyif on WS.

Stole

Begin Old Shale Beg border
With larger circ and using the long-tail cast on, CO 90 sts. Do not join.
First row: (WS) Knit.
Knit 2 more rows.
Work Rows 1–4 of Old Shale Beg seven times.

Change to smaller circ.

Begin Orchard Grass Body
Next row *dec row:* (RS) Sl 1 purlwise wyib, k7, [k2tog, k16] four times, k2tog, k8 (5 sts dec'd)—85 sts rem.
Next row: (WS) Sl 1 purlwise wyif, purl to end.
Work Rows 1–20 of Orchard Grass 13 times.
Next row *inc row:* (RS) Sl 1 purlwise wyib, k7, [m1, k17] four times, m1, k9 (5 sts inc'd)—90 sts.

Change to larger circ.

Begin Old Shale End border
Work Rows 1–4 of Old Shale End seven times.
Next row: (WS) Knit.
Knit 2 more rows.

Next row: (RS) BO all sts knitwise.

Finishing
Weave in ends. Block to measurements

Orchard Grass Chart

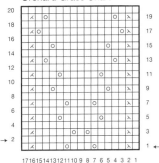

Old Shale Beg Chart

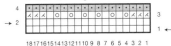

Old Shale End Chart

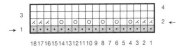

KEY
- ☐ Knit on RS; Purl on WS
- ▪ Purl on RS; Knit on WS
- ◎ YO: Yarn over (1 st increased)
- ⋏ K2tog: Knit 2 together (1 st decreased; leans right)
- ⋌ SSK: Slip, slip, knit (1 st decreased; leans left)
- ☐ Pattern repeat

Camellia Tank
Karen Templer

The minute I first laid eyes on this Camellia Fiber Company handspun, I wanted to wear it, and not just on my head or around my neck. But superbulky can be a challenge to wear and obviously doesn't come cheap, so keeping it spare was the way to go. The resulting sweater is simple and lets the yarn be the star, but there are key details in the knitting that keep the edges tidy — both at the split hem and the armhole edges — even with the thick-and-thin nature of the yarn.

Due to the scale of the stitches, the cast-on edge will be prominent, so be mindful of each stitch as you're casting on and take care to create as consistent and attractive an edge as you can.

Finished measurements
34¾ (37¼, 40, 42¾, 45¼, 48, 50¾, 53¼, 56)" [88.5 (94.5, 101.5, 108.5, 115, 122, 129, 135.5, 142) cm] bust circumference; sample shown in size 37¼" [94.5 cm] with 3¼" [9.5 cm] positive ease Suggested ease: 3" [7.5 cm] to 4" [10 cm] positive ease

Yarn
Patrick Superbulky by Camellia Fiber Company (100% Targhee wool; 4 ounces / 60 yards [55 meters])
• 4 (4, 5, 5, 6, 6, 7, 7, 7) skeins
OR
220 (240, 265, 290, 315, 340, 370, 395, 420) yards [203 (220, 245, 266, 288, 310, 338, 363, 385) meters] of superbulky handspun yarn

Needles
• One 32" [80 cm] circular needle (circ) in size US 19 [15 mm]
• One set double-pointed needles (dpns) in size US 17 [12 mm]
Or size to obtain gauge

Notions
• Waste yarn
• Extra large stitch marker
• 2 locking stitch markers
• Waste yarn or stitch holders
• Tapestry needle

Gauge
6 sts and 10 rnds = 4" [10 cm] in stockinette with larger needles, after blocking.

Notes
Back and front are worked from the bottom up, flat to the split hem, then joined in the round to underarm, then separated again, worked to shoulders, and seamed.

To get an accurate measurement using a thick and thin yarn, measure your gauge over many different places around the swatch, and take the average of the numbers you find.

Larger sizes may wish to use a longer circular needle to accommodate the larger number of stitches.

After completing your tank, if you find the thick-and-thin nature of the yarn has created any too-thin areas in the fabric, use a thicker tail of yarn and work in duplicate stitch to fill in as desired.

Tank
Back Tail
With larger circ and using the long-tail cast on, CO 26 (28, 30, 32, 34, 36, 38, 40, 42) sts. Do not join.
First row: (WS) Purl to last st, k1.

Begin stockinette stitch
Next row: (RS) Sl 1 wyif, knit to last 2 sts, sl 1 wyif, k1.
Next row: Sl 1 wyif, k1, purl to last 2 sts, sl 1 wyif, k1.
Rep the last 2 rows five more times. Place sts onto waste yarn or st holder.

Front tail
With larger circ and using the long-tail cast on, CO 26 (28, 30, 32, 34, 36, 38, 40, 42) sts. Do not join.
First row: (WS) Purl to last st, k1.

Begin stockinette stitch

Next row: (RS) Sl 1 wyif, knit to last 2 sts,
sl 1 wyif, k1.
Next row: Sl 1 wyif, k1, purl to last 2 sts,
sl 1 wyif, k1.
Rep the last 2 rows three more times.

Join front and back

Next row: (RS) K1, k1-tbl, knit to end, with RS
facing return sts for back to LH needle, then k1,
k1-tbl, knit to end. Pm for BOR and join to work in
the rnd—52 (56, 60, 64, 68, 72, 76, 80, 84) sts
on needle.
Next rnd: Knit.
Cont in St st until pc meas approx 10¾" [27.5 cm]
from beg, measured in the front. Place sts for front
onto waste yarn or st holder—26 (28, 30, 32, 34,
36, 38, 40, 42) sts rem for back.
Pin a removable marker in one stitch (or run a
piece of waste yarn through a few stitches) 6 or 8"
[15.5 or 20.5 cm] from one edge, on both Front
and Back, to mark the separation row.

Back

Next row: (WS) Purl to last st, turn work.

Begin sloped bind off armhole shaping

Next row *dec row:* (RS) Sl 1 st purlwise to RH
needle, then pass rem st from previous row over st,
knit to last st, turn work (1 st dec'd)—25 (27, 29,
31, 33, 35, 37, 39, 41) sts.
Next row *dec row:* Sl 1 st purlwise to RH needle,
then pass rem st from previous row over st, purl to
last st, turn work (1 st dec'd)—24 (26, 28, 30, 32,
34, 36, 38, 40) sts.
Rep the last 2 rows 2 (2, 3, 3, 4, 4, 5, 5, 6) more
times, purling to end on final row—20 (22, 22, 24,
24, 26, 26, 28, 28) sts rem.

Continue in stockinette stitch

Row 1: (RS) Sl 1 wyif, knit to last 2 sts,
sl 1 wyif, k1.
Row 2: (WS) Sl 1 wyif, k1, purl to last 2 sts,
sl 1 wyif, k1.

Rep the last 2 rows until back meas approx 8 (8½,
8¾, 9, 9¼, 9½, 10, 10½, 10¾)" [20.5 (21.5, 22,
23, 23.5, 24, 25.5, 26.5, 27.5) cm] from
separation row.
Next row: BO all sts.

Front

Transfer sts held for front to circ. Join yarn ready to
work a WS row.
Work front same as for back until front meas approx 4¼ (4¾, 5, 5¼, 5¼, 5½, 6, 6, 6¼)" [11 (12,
12.5, 13.5, 13.5, 14, 15, 15, 16) cm] from separation row, ending after a WS row.

Begin neck shaping

Next row: (RS) Work 7 (8, 8, 9, 9, 9, 9, 10, 10) sts
as est, then place these sts onto waste yarn or st
holder, BO 6 (6, 6, 6, 6, 8, 8, 8, 8) sts, work as est
to end.

Right Front

Next row: (WS) Work as est to last st, turn work.
Next row *dec row:* (RS) Sl 1 st purlwise to RH
needle, then pass rem st from previous row over st,
work as est to end (1 st dec'd)—6 (7, 7, 8, 8, 8, 8,
9, 9) sts rem.
Rep the last 2 rows one more time—5 (6, 6, 7, 7,
7, 7, 8, 8) sts rem.
Cont in St st as est until front meas same as back.
Next row: BO all sts.

Left Front

Transfer sts held for right front to circ. Join yarn
ready to work a WS row.
Next row: (WS) Purl to last 2 sts, sl 1 wyif, k1.
Next row: (RS) Work as est to last st, turn work.
Next row *dec row:* (WS) Sl 1 st purlwise to RH
needle, then pass rem st from previous row over st,
work as est to end (1 st dec'd)—6 (7, 7, 8, 8, 8, 8,
9, 9) sts rem.
Rep the last 2 rows one more time—5 (6, 6, 7, 7,
7, 7, 8, 8) sts rem.
Cont in St st as est until front meas same as back.
Next row: BO all sts.

Finishing

Weave in ends. Block to measurements.
Sew front shoulders to corresponding sts on back.

Neckband

Using smaller dpns and beg at left shoulder seam, pick up and knit 10 (10, 10, 10, 10, 12, 12, 12, 12) sts along edge of back neck, pick up and knit 6 (6, 6, 6, 6, 6, 6, 8, 8) sts along left side of front neck edge, pick up and knit 6 (6, 6, 6, 6, 8, 8, 8, 8) sts along front neck sts, then pick up and knit 6 (6, 6, 6, 6, 6, 6, 8, 8) sts along right side of front neck edge—28 (28, 28, 28, 28, 32, 32, 36, 36) sts on needles. Pm for BOR.

Begin rib

Next rnd: P1; *k2, p2; rep from * to last 3 sts, k2, p1.
Cont in rib for 3 more rnds.
Next rnd: BO loosely in pattern.

Karen is the blogger behind Fringe Association (fringeassociation.com) and the owner of Fringe Supply Co. (fringesupplyco.com). She lives in Nashville TN. Instagram: fringesupplyco

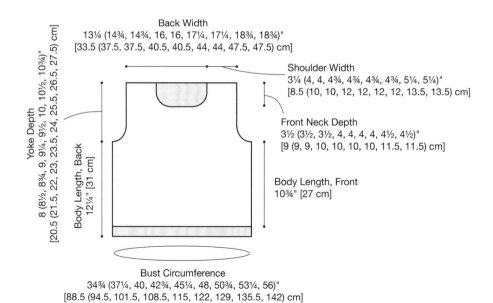

Yoke Depth
8 (8½, 8¾, 9, 9¼, 9½, 10, 10½, 10¾)"
[20.5 (21.5, 22, 23, 23.5, 24, 25.5, 26.5, 27.5) cm]

Back Width
13¼ (14¾, 14¾, 16, 16, 17¼, 17¼, 18¾, 18¾)"
[33.5 (37.5, 37.5, 40.5, 40.5, 44, 44, 47.5, 47.5) cm]

Shoulder Width
3¼ (4, 4, 4¾, 4¾, 4¾, 4¾, 5¼, 5¼)"
[8.5 (10, 10, 12, 12, 12, 12, 13.5, 13.5) cm]

Front Neck Depth
3½ (3½, 3½, 4, 4, 4, 4, 4½, 4½)"
[9 (9, 9, 10, 10, 10, 10, 11.5, 11.5) cm]

Body Length, Front
10¾" [27 cm]

Body Length, Back
12¼" [31 cm]

Bust Circumference
34¾ (37¼, 40, 42¾, 45¼, 48, 50¾, 53¼, 56)"
[88.5 (94.5, 101.5, 108.5, 115, 122, 129, 135.5, 142) cm]

Doe Cap
Jenny Gordy

I designed this hat for my daughter to wear on her first Halloween several years ago. Since then I've enjoyed knitting this simple pattern again and again, experimenting with different ear shapes for different animals. We keep them in the dress-up box year round for imaginative play and sometimes they make their way into her daily winter hat rotation.

Finished measurements
6 (6½, 7, 7½, 8, 8½)" [15 (16.5, 18, 19, 20.5, 21.5) cm] length from front edge to back of head
5½ (6, 6½, 7, 7¾, 8¼)" [14 (15, 16.5, 18, 19.5, 21) cm] width from neck edge to top of hat
To fit: 14½-15½ (15½-16½, 16½-17½, 17½-18½, 18½-19½, 19½-20½)" [37–39 (39.5–42, 42–44.5, 44.5–47, 47–49.5, 49.5–52) cm] head circumference
Size guide: 0-3m (3-6m, 6-12m, 12-24m, 4y, 6y)
Sample shown in 12–24m size

Yarn
Alpaca Elegance by Green Mountain Spinnery (50% Alpaca, 50% Wool; 58 grams / 180 yards [165 meters])
• 1 (1, 1, 1, 1, 2) skein(s) in Chai
OR
84 (104, 123, 147, 167, 186) yards [77 (95, 112, 134, 153, 170) meters] of dk weight yarn

Needles
• One 16" [40.5 cm] circular (circ) in size US 5 [3.75 mm]
• One set of 4 double-pointed needles (dpns) in size US 5 [3.75 mm]
• One 16" circ in size US 4 [3.5 mm]
Or sizes to obtain gauge

Notions
• Stitch markers
• Tapestry needle

Gauge
24 sts and 32 rows/rnds = 4" [10 cm] in stockinette stitch with larger needles, after blocking.

Applied I-Cord: With 2 sts already on needle, pick up and knit 1 st along edge—3 sts. *Without turning the work, slip all sts to the right end of needle. Pull yarn tightly from the end of the row, k1, k2tog-tbl—2 sts rem. Pick up and knit 1 st along edge—3 sts; rep from * to end.

Notes
The hat begins by knitting back and forth in rows, then the stitches are joined and worked in the round for a little ways before beginning the crown shaping. The crown is decreased. The first I-cord tie is knit and attached to the opening in the hat, and the second I-cord tie is knit. Ears are knit and sewn to the top of the hat.

Hat
With smaller circ and using the long-tail cast on, CO 72 (78, 84, 90, 96, 102) sts. Do not join.

Begin ribbing
Row 1: (WS) *K1, p1; rep from * to end.
Row 2: *K1, p1; rep from * to end.
Rep last 2 rows until pc meas 1" [2.5 cm] from CO edge, ending with a WS row.
Change to larger circ.

Begin stockinette stitch
Next row: (RS) Knit.
Next row: Purl.
Cont in St st until hat meas 3¼ (3½, 3¾, 4, 4¼, 4¾)" [8.5 (9, 9.5, 10, 11, 12) cm] from beg, ending after a RS row.
Place marker (pm) for beg of rnd and join to work in the rnd.

Begin stockinette stitch in the rnd
Next row: Knit.
Cont working in St st in the rnd until hat meas 3¾ (4¼, 4½, 5, 5½, 6)" [9.5 (11, 11.5, 12.5, 14, 15) cm] from beg.

Begin crown shaping

Note: Change to dpns when sts no longer fit comfortably on circ.

Next rnd *set-up rnd:* *K2tog, k8 (9, 10, 11, 12, 13), ssk, pm; rep from * five more times (12 sts dec'd)—60 (66, 72, 78, 84, 90) sts rem. Knit 3 rnds.

Next rnd *dec rnd:* *K2tog, knit to 2 sts before m, ssk, sl m; rep from * five more times (12 sts dec'd)—48 (54, 60, 66, 72, 78) sts rem.

Rep *dec rnd* every 4th rnd one more time, then every other rnd 2 (2, 3, 3, 4, 4) more times—12 (18, 12, 18, 12, 18) sts rem. Remove st markers.

Next rnd *dec rnd:* *K2tog; rep from * to end— 6 (9, 6, 9, 6, 9) sts rem.

Finishing

Cut yarn and use a tapestry needle to thread tail through the last sts on the needles. Remove needles from work and cinch hole at the end of the hat closed. Thread the tail through to the inside of the hat and weave in ends.

Neck Ties

With dpns, CO 2 sts. Knit I-cord (see page 152) for 12". With same needle your knitting is on, pick up and knit every st around the selvedge edge of flat St st section of the hat, applying I-cord as you go. Cont knitting 12" of I-cord. BO 2 st. Weave in ends. Knot the ends of each cord.

Ears

With dpns, CO 16 (20, 24, 28, 28, 28) sts. Divide sts evenly over 3 dpns. Pm for beg of rnd and join to work in the rnd, being careful not to twist sts.

Shape Ear

Knit 4 rnds.

Next rnd *inc rnd:* K4 (5, 6, 7, 7, 7), m1, k8 (10, 12, 14, 14, 14), m1, k4 (5, 6, 7, 7, 7) sts (2 sts inc'd)—18 (22, 26, 30, 30, 30) sts. Knit 3 rnds.

Next rnd *inc rnd:* K4 (5, 6, 7, 7, 7), m1, k10 (12, 14, 16, 16, 16), m1, k4 (5, 6, 7, 7, 7) sts (2 sts inc'd)—20 (24, 28, 32, 32, 32) sts. Knit 3 rnds.

Next rnd *set-up rnd:* K2tog, k6 (8, 10, 12, 12, 12), ssk, pm, k2tog, k6 (8, 10, 12, 12, 12), ssk (4 sts dec'd)—16 (20, 24, 28, 28, 28) sts rem. Knit 1 rnd.

Next rnd *dec rnd:* *K2tog, knit to 2 sts before m, ssk, sl m; rep from * to end (4 sts dec'd)— 12 (16, 20, 24, 24, 24) sts rem.

Next rnd: Knit.

Rep the last 2 rnds 1 (2, 3, 4, 4, 4) more time(s)— 8 sts rem.

Cut yarn and thread tail through the last sts on the needles. Remove needles and cinch hole closed. Thread the tail through to the inside of the ear and weave in the end. Leave the tail long at the bottom of the ear for sewing the ear to the hat. Rep for second ear.

Attach Ears

Fold ear in half along the bottom edge. The decreases at the top of the ear should be in the center. One ear will be placed along the 3rd set of crown decreases on the hat, the front edge of the ear lined up with the beginning of the decreases. The second ear will be placed along the 5th set of decreases. Sew the ears to the hat and weave in the ends on the inside of the hat.

Block to measurements.

Jenny is a knitwear designer & a sewing pattern maker living in Portland, OR.
www.shopwiksten.com Instagram: shopwiksten

Butterfly & Cocoon
Susan B. Anderson

Late summer into early fall is a completely magical time here in Wisconsin. On my daily hikes through the prairies with grasses towering over my head, and around nearby ponds surrounded by milkweed, the terrain is intoxicating. These natural habitats offer a huge variety of fauna-watching, including wild turkeys, deer, chipmunks, herons, cranes, birds galore, and my favorite, the butterflies. Oh the butterflies! To see their beautiful, airy wings flitting about in abundance from plant to plant has added so much to my daily excursions. Each walk in the fading heat of the season is a heady experience.

Butterfly & Cocoon is a knitted tribute to these beautiful, delicate creatures. The sweet butterfly and cocoon are both worked seamlessly from the bottom-up, picking up stitches for the wings and antennae after the body is knitted. This makes for a slick and fun knit. Children will love to tuck the winged friend into its very own cocoon for a rest or nap and take it out again when it's time to fly! The loop on the top of the cocoon hood is perfect for hanging on a hook, backpack or most definitely on a little finger for toting along on adventures in the wild.

Finished measurements
5½" [14 cm] tall
Yarn
Chickadee by Quince & Co.
(100% American wool; 50 grams / 181 yards [166 meters])
• 1 skein each (only small amounts of each color are used) in the following colorways:

Sample 1: Kumlien's Gull (A), Egret (B), Shell (C), Split Pea (D)
Sample 2: Clay (A), Chanterelle (B), Aleutian (C), Honey (D)
Sample 3: Iceland (A), Petal (B), Lupine (C), Pomegranate (D)
OR
50 yards [46 meters] or less of each color in sport weight yarn
Needles
For Butterfly:
• One set of double-pointed needles in US size 3 [3.25 mm]
For Cocoon:
• One set of double-pointed needles in US size 5 [3.75 mm]
Or sizes to obtain gauge
Notions
• Tapestry needle
• Removable stitch markers
• Fiberfill
• Safety eyes, size 4.5 mm [see Notes]
• Black embroidery floss
• Waste yarn
Gauge
6½ sts = 1" [2.5 cm] in stockinette stitch with smaller needles
6 sts = 1" [2.5 cm] in stockinette stitch with larger needles

Notes
Butterfly is worked in the round from the bottom up and stuffed as you go. Face detail, wings, and antennae are added after. Cocoon is worked from the bottom up in the round, then bound off at beginning of hood and continued in garter stitch. Top of hood is grafted, with stitches kept live at center of hood to make I-cord loop.
Warning: Safety eyes are considered a choking hazard for young children and infants. Embroider eyes if this is a concern.

Butterfly

Begin at bottom

With Color A, smaller dpns, and using the long-tail cast on, CO 9 sts. Divide evenly onto 3 dpns. Place a locking st marker into first st for BOR and join to work in the rnd.

Shape lower body

Rnds 1-3: Knit.
Rnd 4 *inc rnd:* *K1, [m1, k1] two times; rep from * to end (6 sts inc'd)—15 sts.
Rnds 5-7: Knit.
Rnd 8 *inc rnd:* *K1, m1, k3, m1, k1; rep from * to end (6 sts inc'd)—21 sts.
Rnds 9 and 10: Knit.
Rnd 11 *inc rnd:* *K3, k1-f/b, k3; rep from * to end (3 sts inc'd)—24 sts.
Rnds 12-15: Knit.
Rnd 16 *dec rnd:* *K2, k2tog; rep from * to end (6 sts dec'd)—18 sts rem.
Rnd 17: Knit.
Rnd 18 *dec rnd:* *K2, k2tog, k2; rep from * to end (3 sts dec'd)—15 sts rem.

Thread tail from CO onto tapestry needle. Thread through CO sts, gather and cinch closed. Draw yarn to inside of doll. Stuff the body with fiberfill. Change to Color B, but leave Color A attached.

Shape upper body

Work upper body in stripes: two rows of Color B, two rows Color A, carrying yarn loosely along inside of body.
Rnd 1: Knit.
Rnd 2 *inc rnd:* *[K1, m1] four times, k1; rep from * to end (12 sts inc'd)—27 sts total.
Rnd 3: Knit.
Rnd 4 *inc rnd:* *K2, k1-f/b; rep from * to end (9 sts inc'd)—36 sts.
Rnds 5-19: Knit. On Rnd 9, place a locking st marker in a st near BOR and leave it there for wing placement.
Rnd 20 *dec rnd:* *K2tog; rep from * to end— 18 sts rem.

Break Color A. Draw yarn to inside of doll. Stuff upper body with fiberfill. Cont with Color B.

Shape head

Rnd 1: Knit.
Rnd 2 *inc rnd:* *K1-f/b; rep from * to end (18 sts inc'd)—36 sts.
Rnd 3: Knit.
Rnd 4 *inc rnd:* *K5, k1-f/b; rep from * to end (6 sts inc'd)—42 sts.
Rnds 5–18: Knit. On Rnd 10: If using safety eyes, place safety eyes on 17th and 26th stitches, then cont in St st. If embroidering eyes, place a locking stitch marker in a stitch on opposite side of head from BOR on Rnd 10 and leave in place for eye placement.

Rnd 19 *dec rnd:* *K5, k2tog; rep from * to end (6 sts dec'd)—36 sts rem.
Rnd 20: Knit.
Rnd 21 *dec rnd:* *K4, k2tog; rep from * to end— 30 sts rem.
Rnd 22: Knit.
Rnd 23 *dec rnd:* *K3, k2tog; rep from * to end— 24 sts rem.
Rnd 24: Knit.
Rnd 25 *dec rnd:* *K2, k2tog; rep from * to end— 18 sts rem.

Stuff the head with fiberfill. When you are stuffing the head be sure to push out on the sides of the fabric to form the head in a round shape.

Tip: Always use small tufts or pinches of the fiberfill at a time when stuffing toys. Never use large clumps of stuffing at one time. You want to break up the fiberfill.

Rnd 26: Knit.
Rnd 27 *dec rnd:* *K2tog; rep from * to end— 9 sts rem.

Break yarn and thread onto tapestry needle. Draw through rem sts and cinch closed.
Draw the ends to the inside of the doll and trim.

Embroidered Eyes

If you are embroidering eyes, locate the center front of the face as noted by the locking stitch marker you placed on Rnd 10 of the head. With a length of black embroidery floss and tapestry needle, make two French knots on the row marked while shaping head, evenly spaced in each direction from center.

Mouth

With a length of black embroidery floss and tapestry needle, make two straight stitches to form a V centered in between the eyes, with the point of the V on the 5th rnd up from the start of the head.

First wing

With smaller dpn, beg at BOR of row marked in upper body, count 10 sts to the left and starting here, pick up 8 sts (inserting needle under the right leg of each stich, one above the last). With second dpn and working 1 st to the left of the pick up row, pick up 8 more sts in the same manner—16 sts on needles. Join Color C at lower edge of front needle.
Rnd 1: Knit. As you work, arrange the sts as follows:
Needle 1: 8 sts.
Needles 2 and 3: 4 sts each.
Rnd 2 inc rnd: Needle 1: K1-f/b, knit to last st, k1-f/b. **Needle 2:** K1-f/b, knit to end. **Needle 3:** Knit to last st, k1-f/b (4 sts inc'd)—20 sts.
Rnd 3: Knit.
Rep Rnds 2 and 3 two more times, the work Rnd 2 once more—32 sts on needles.

Split wing

Rnd 1: K8, then place the next 16 sts onto waste yarn, knit rem 8 sts—16 sts rem.
Cont in the rnd on 2 dpns.
Rnd 2 dec rnd: *Ssk, k4, k2tog; rep from * for second needle (4 sts dec'd)—12 sts rem.
Rnd 3: Knit.
Rnd 4 dec rnd: *Ssk, k2, k2tog; rep from * for second needle (4 sts dec'd)—8 sts rem.
Rnd 5: Knit.

Break yarn and thread onto tapestry needle. Draw through rem sts and cinch closed.

Transfer 16 held sts to 2 dpns. Join yarn and work same as for other wing half.

Second wing

With smaller dpn, beg at BOR of row marked in upper body, count 10 sts to the right and starting here, pick up 8 sts (inserting needle under the right leg of each stich, one above the last). With second dpn and working 1 st to the right of the pick up row, pick up 8 more sts in the same manner—16 sts on needles. Join Color C at lower edge of front needle.

Work second wing same as for first.
Draw all ends to the inside of the doll and trim. Pull and shape wings so they have a rounded shape.

Right Antenna

With a smaller dpn, count 10 rows above the right eye, then count 3 sts to the right. Pick up these 3 sts by inserting needle tip under the right leg of each st. Join Color C, leaving a 15" [38 cm] tail for wrapping later.

Work 6 rows of I-cord.

Next row inc row: (K1-f/b) three times—6 sts on needles. Divide evenly onto 3 dpns.
Knit 2 rnds.

Take a very tiny pinch of fiberfill and roll it in your hand until it is the size of a small pea. Tuck the ball inside the end of the antenna. Break yarn and thread onto tapestry needle. Draw through sts and cinch closed. Tightly wrap antenna with long tail, beginning at head, working up to stuffed end, then wrapping back down again. Draw ends to the inside of antenna and head and trim. Form the antenna so it has a curved shape going outward from the side of the face.

Left Antenna

With a smaller dpn, count 10 rows above the left eye, then count 3 sts to the left. Pick up these 3 sts by inserting needle tip under the right leg of each st. Join Color C, leaving a 15" [38 cm] tail for wrapping later.

Work left antenna same as for right.

Cocoon

With Color D, larger dpns, and using the long-tail cast on, CO 9 sts and divide evenly onto 3 dpns. Place a locking st marker into first st for BOR and join to work in the rnd.

Begin at bottom

Rnds 1-4: Knit.
Rnd 5 *inc rnd:* *K1, [k1, m1] two times; rep from * to end (6 sts inc'd)—15 sts.
Rnds 6-8: Knit.
Rnd 9 *inc rnd:* *K1, m1, k3, m1, k1; rep from * to end (6 sts inc'd)—21 sts.
Rnds 10 and 11: Knit.
Rnd 12 *inc rnd:* *K3, k1-f/b, k3; rep from * to end (3 sts inc'd)—24 sts.
Rnds 13 and 14: Knit.
Rnd 15 *inc rnd:* *K1, m1, k6, m1, k1; rep from * to end (6 sts inc'd)—30 sts.
Rnds 16 and 17: Knit.
Rnd 18 *inc rnd:* *K1, m1, k8, m1, k1; rep from * to end (6 sts inc'd)—36 sts.
Rnds 19 and 20: Knit.
Rnd 21 *inc rnd:* *K3, k1-f/b; rep from * to end (9 sts inc'd)—45 sts.
Rnds 22-35: Knit.
Rnd 36 *dec rnd:* *K3, k2tog; rep from * to end (9 sts dec'd)—36 sts rem.
Rnds 37–39: *K1, p1; rep from * to end.
Rnd 40: K15, BO 6 sts, knit to end—30 sts rem.

Hood

Keep 15 sts each on 2 dpns while working back and forth until it is comfortable to work with all sts on one needle.
Knit to BO edge, turn.

Tip: To close the gap from starting the bind off mid-row, pick up the front leg of the first bound-off stitch and place on RH needle. When working first row, knit it together with the next st on needle.

Next row: (WS) Knit.
Knit every row until there are 12 garter ridges visible on the RS, ending after a WS row.

Next row *dec row:* (RS) K9, (k2tog) six times, k9—24 sts rem.
Break yarn leaving a 48" [122 cm] tail. Divide sts evenly on two dpns.
With WS together use the Kitchener stitch to join sides of hood until 3 sts rem on each needle.
Knit the first st of each needle together. Rep two more times—3 sts rem.

I-cord loop

Next row *dec row:* K2tog, k1—2 sts rem.
Work in I-cord for 2" [5 cm].
Next row *dec row:* K2tog.
Break yarn and draw through rem st. Thread tail onto tapestry needle. Form I-cord into a loop and tack down 2-3 sts to keep in place.

Finishing

Weave in ends. Steam-block Cocoon to even sts.

Fold the wings over the belly of the Butterfly before inserting into the Cocoon.
Have fun and enjoy!

Susan is a knitwear designer, instructor, blogger and author living in Madison, WI. She spends her days creating fun-to-knit patterns, getting outside in the wilds of Wisconsin and enjoying her big family.
www.susanbanderson.blogspot.com
Instagram: susanbanderson

Sea Urchin Treasure Bag
by Mary Jane Mucklestone

When I go to the beach I inevitably bring home rocks and shells and other treasures. One of the most delicate finds are elegant pale green, almost grey, sea urchin shells. This treasure bag will be just the thing for toting them home in one piece, the softness of the wool protecting them.

Finished measurements
13¼" [33.5 cm] circumference and
8.25" [21 cm] length
Yarn
Tide by Starcroft Fiber Mill
(100% Maine wool; 50 grams / 175 yards
[162 meters])
- 1 skein in Driftwood (MC)
- 1 skein in Cove (CC)
OR
MC: 77 yards [70 meters]; CC: 47 yards
[43 meters] in DK weight yarn
Needles
- One 16" [40 cm] circular needle (circ) in size US 3 [3.25 mm]
- One set double-pointed needles (dpns) in size US 3 [3.25 mm]
- One set dpns in size US 8 [5 mm] (optional; for I-cord tie)
Or size to obtain gauge
Notions
- One crochet hook in size US 4/E [3.5 mm] and smooth waste yarn for the provisional cast on
- Stitch markers
- Tapestry needle
Gauge
24 sts and 30 rnds = 4" [10 cm] in Sea Urchin Chart, after blocking.

Helpful Links
There are many YouTube videos illustrating the provisional cast-on technique. Purl Soho also has a good one: www.purlsoho.com/create/2015/04/03/provisional-cast-on-video/

There are also handy YouTube videos that describe a butterfly stitch with gimp for making lanyards. The procedure is very similar to making the finger crochet cord, only we use our finger to grab the loops. www.youtube.com/watch?v=Hh6vThlt2Fk

Bag
Using the crochet hook and waste yarn, CO 80 sts onto the circ. With MC, knit 1 row. Pm for beg of rnd and join to work in the rnd, being careful not to twist sts.

Knit 10 rnds.
Join CC and work Rnds 1–36 of the Sea Urchin Chart. Break CC.
Knit 8 rnds.

Edging
Next rnd: Purl.
Next rnd: Knit.
Next rnd: Purl.
Next rnd *tie hole rnd:* *K5, BO 2 sts, k3; rep from * seven more times.
Next rnd: *P5, using the backwards loop cast on, CO 2 sts, p3; rep from * seven more times.
Next rnd: Knit.
Next rnd: Purl.
Rep last 2 rnds one time.

Next rnd: Loosely BO all sts.

Base
Carefully unzip the provisional CO and place 80 sts onto dpns. Pm for beg of rnd and join to work in the rnd.

First rnd: With CC, knit.

Begin base shaping
Next rnd *set-up rnd:* *P10, pm; rep from * seven more times times, knit to end (BOR is final shaping marker).

Next rnd *dec rnd:* *Knit to 2 sts before m, k2tog; rep from * seven more times (8 sts dec'd)— 72 sts rem.

Rep *dec rnd* every 3rd rnd three more times, then every other rnd 4 times—16 sts rem.

Next rnd *dec rnd:* *K2tog; rep from * 7 more times—8 sts rem.

Break yarn. With tapestry needle thread through remaining loops.

Finishing

Weave in ends. Wet block over a Mason Jar or other cylindrical item.

Finger crochet or "butterfly stitch" cord or knit an I-Cord. Make sure you use *two strands together*, for added strength, when making your tie.

Butterfly Stitch Finger Crochet Tie

Make a slip knot using CC (#1) and hang the loop loosely from your left index finger.

Hold another doubled strand of CC (#2) in your left hand alongside the other.

Using your right index finger, draw a loop of strand #2 through the slip knot loop, and drop the slip knot from your left finger. Pull the slip knot tight. Draw a loop of strand #1 through the loop on your right index finger with your left index finger, and drop the loop from your right finger. Pull the right hand loop tight.

Repeat this process of drawing loops through and pulling tight until lanyard is 40" [102cm] or desired length. Cut the ends and pull the end of one color completely through the loop of the other to finish.

I-cord Tie

With CC and larger dpns, CO 4 sts. *Knit all sts. Slide the sts to the other end of the needle without turning and pull yarn across the back; rep from * until your cord is 40" [102 cm] or desired length, then BO all sts.

Thread Tie

Beginning at the join, thread the cord through the eight holes of the treasure bag twice. Knot the two ends of the cord together. Pull out the cord at the other side to form a loop, creating a draw-string effect.

Go out and find some treasures!

Sea Urchin Chart

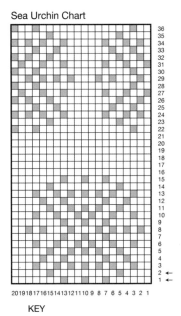

20 19 18 17 16 15 14 13 12 11 10 9 8 7 6 5 4 3 2 1

KEY

☐ With MC, knit

▨ With CC, knit

☐ Pattern repeat

Byssus Cocoon
by Bristol Ivy

I am a girl of the sea. I am not content unless I'm near the ocean, and every home I've ever lived in has been liberally festooned with the treasures I've brought back from the shore. Some of my favorites of these, nestled in among the seaglass and tumbled quartz, are the gently textured and curved clam and mussel shells. The Byssus Cocoon is an homage to their effortless curves and delicate texture, and is perfect for a late evening wander along the waterline.

Finished measurements
32¼ (33¾, 37¼, 39¾)" [82 (85.5, 94.5, 101) cm] back width, to fit bust size 30-36 (36¼-42¼, 42½-48½, 48¾-54¾)" [76-91.5 (92-107.5, 108-123, 124-129) cm]; shown in size 32¼" [82 cm] on a 35" model

Yarn
Hayton 4-ply by Eden Cottage Yarns (80% merino, 10% cashmere, 10% nylon; 100 grams / 380 yards [347 meters])
• 3 (4, 4, 4) skeins in Stone
OR
1050 (1155, 1325, 1460) yards [958 (1054, 1209, 1334) meters] in fingering weight yarn

Needles
• One 32" [80 cm] circular needle (circ) in size US 6 [4 mm]
• Two double-pointed needles in size US 6 [4 mm]
Or size to obtain gauge

Notions
• Crochet hook and waste yarn
• Stitch markers
• Locking stitch markers
• Stitch holders or waste yarn
• Tapestry needle

Gauge
23 sts and 31 rows = 4" [10 cm] in stockinette stitch, after blocking.

Notes
Shrug begins at the center of lower back, working lace band out in both directions from a provisional cast on. Band stitches are held while back stitches are picked up and worked to shoulder. Stitches are picked up along lower side of back stitches and worked along with held lace band to form fronts with lace detail and pleats. Front bound off edge is seamed to remaining upper side edge and bound off edge of back. Front lace bands are continued and sewn down along back neck.

Lace Panel
Row 1: (RS) P1, k2tog, (yo) twice, ssk, p1.
Row 2: (WS) K1, p1, [k1, p1] into double yo, p1, k1.
Row 3: P1, yo, ssk, k2tog, yo, p1.
Row 4: K1, p4, k1.
Rep Rows 1–4 for Lace Panel.

Garter rib
Row 1: (RS) Knit.
Row 2: (WS) Purl.
Rows 3 and 4: Knit.
Rep Rows 1–4 for Garter ridge.

Cocoon
Band
With waste yarn and the crochet provisional cast on, CO 8 sts.

Begin Left Band
First row: (WS) P1, k1, p4, k1, p1.

Begin Lace Panel
Row 1: (RS) K1, work Row 1 of Lace Panel to last st, k1.
Row 2: (WS) P1, work Row 2 of Lace Panel to last st, p1.
Cont in lace panel as est until pc meas 17¼ (18, 19¾, 21)" [44 (45.5, 49.5, 53.5) cm] from beg, ending after Row 3 of Lace Panel.
Next row: (WS) P1, k1, p4, ssk (1 st dec'd)—7 sts rem.

Break yarn and place sts onto waste yarn or st holder.

Right Band

Unzip provisional CO and place 8 live sts on needle. Join yarn ready to work a WS row.
Work Right Band same as for Left Band, working final row as follows:
Next row: (WS) K2tog, p4, k1, p1 (1 st dec'd)—7 sts rem.
Place sts onto waste yarn or st holder; do not break yarn.

Band

With RS facing so that Right Band with attached yarn is on the RH side, with a new ball of yarn, pick up and knit 186 (194, 214, 228) sts along top edge of band. Do not join to Lace Panel.
Next row: (WS) P82 (86, 96, 103), pm, k1, p4, k1, pm, p10, pm, k1, p4, k1, pm, p82 (86, 96, 103).

Begin stockinette and lace and garter panels

Next row: (RS) Knit to m, sl m, work Row 1 of Lace Panel, sl m, work Row 1 of Garter ridge to next m, sl m, work Row 1 of Lace Panel, sl m, knit to end.
Next row: Purl to m, sl m, work Row 2 of Lace Panel, sl m, work Row 2 of Garter ridge, sl m, work Row 2 of Lace Panel, sl m, purl to end.
Cont in St st, lace panels, and Garter ridge until pc meas 10½ (11, 11¾, 12¼)" [26.5 (28, 30, 31) cm] from pick up edge, ending after a WS row. Place a locking stitch marker into the stitch at each side of last row for shoulder seam placement.

Begin Back shaping

Next row *dec row:* (RS) K1, ssk, work as est to last 3 sts, k2tog, k1 (2 sts dec'd)—184 (192, 212, 226) sts rem.
Rep *dec row* every RS row 28 (31, 34, 36) more times—128 (130, 144, 154) sts rem.
Work 1 WS row.

Begin shoulder shaping

Next row: (RS) BO 5 (5, 6, 6) sts knitwise, work as est to end—123 (125, 138, 148) sts rem.
Next row: BO 5 (5, 6, 6) sts purlwise, work as est to end—118 (120, 132, 142) sts rem.
Rep the last 2 rows five more times—68 (70, 72, 82) rem.

Next row: (RS) BO rem sts knitwise. Place a locking stitch marker on each side of final bind off row for shoulder seam placement.

Right Front

Return sts held for right band to circ. With attached yarn, k1, work Row 1 of Lace Panel, then pick up and knit 56 (58, 62, 65) sts along side edge of back to marker—63 (65, 69, 72) sts on needle.
Next row: (WS) K4, p16 (18, 22, 25), pm, *k1, p4, k1, pm, p12, pm; rep from * one more time, work Row 2 of Lace Panel, p1.

Begin stitch patterns and front shaping

Next row *inc row:* (RS) K1, *work Row 3 of Lace Panel, sl m, work Row 3 of Garter ridge, sl m; rep from * one more time, work Row 3 of Lace Panel, sl m, knit to last 4 sts, m1-L, k4. (1 st inc'd)—64 (66, 70, 73) sts.
Next row: (WS) K4, purl to m, sl m, *work Row 4 of Lace Panel, sl m, work Row 4 of Garter ridge, sl m; rep from * one more time, work Row 4 of Lace Panel, p1.
Rep *inc row* every RS row 24 (21, 18, 16) more times, then every 4 rows 11 (14, 17, 19) times—99 (101, 105, 108) sts.
Work 1 WS row.

Pleats

Next row: (RS) Removing markers in pleat sections as you come to them, k1, work Lace Panel, sl m, *sl next 6 sts onto a dpn, sl next 6 sts onto a second dpn, fold the dpns toward you so that the RS of the middle dpn is facing the work on the needle and the RS of the outer dpn is facing you, knit together the first st of each dpn and the first st on LH needle (3 sts total), repeat until all 6 sts from each dpn have been worked; rep from * one more time, work as est to end—75 (77, 81, 84) sts rem.
Next row: (WS) BO purlwise to 1 st before m, p1, remove m, work Lace Panel, p1—6 sts rem.

Begin Neck Band

Next row: (RS) K1, work Lace Panel, k1.
Next row: (WS) P1, work Lace Panel, p1.

Cont as est until band meas 4½ (4½, 4¾, 5¼)" [11.5 (11.5, 12, 13.5) cm] from shoulder BO, ending after Row 3 of Lace Panel. Break yarn and place sts onto waste yarn or st holder.

Left Front
With RS of back facing, beg at lower shoulder marker of left back, pick up and knit 56 (58, 62, 65) sts along side of lower back to held band sts, place band sts onto LH needle, then work Row 1 of Lace Panel, k1—63 (65, 69, 72) sts on needle.
Next row: (WS) P1, work Row 2 of Lace Panel, pm, *p12, pm, k1, p4, k1, pm; rep from * one more time, p16 (18, 22, 25), k4.

Next row inc row: (RS) K4, m1-R, knit to m, sl m, *work Row 3 of Lace panel, sl m, work Row 3 of Garter ridge, sl m; rep from * one more time, work Row 3 of Lace Panel, k1 (1 st inc'd)—64 (66, 70, 73) sts.
Next row: (WS) P1, *work Row 4 of Lace Panel, sl m, work Row 4 of Garter ridge, sl m; rep from * one more time, work Row 4 of Lace Panel, purl to last 4 sts, k4.
Rep inc row every RS row 24 (21, 18, 16) more times, then every 4 rows 11 (14, 17, 19) times— 99 (101, 105, 108) sts.

Pleats
Next row: (WS) Removing markers in pleat sections as you come to them, p1, work lace panel, sl m, *sl next 6 sts onto a dpn, sl next 6 sts onto a second dpn, fold the dpns away you so that the RS of the middle dpn is facing the RS of the work on the needle, the RS of the outer dpn is facing away from you, and the knitting closest to you is the WS of the working needle, purl together the first st of each dpn and the first st on LH needle (3 sts total), repeat until all 6 sts from each dpn have been worked; rep from * one more time, work as est to end—75 (77, 81, 84) sts rem.
Next row: (RS) BO knitwise to 1 st before m, p1, remove m, work Lace panel, k1.

Begin Neck Band
Next row: (WS) P1, work Lace Panel, p1.
Next row: (RS) K1, work Lace Panel, k1.
Cont as est until band meas 4½ (4½, 4¾, 5¼)" [11.5 (11.5, 12, 13.5) cm] from shoulder BO, ending after Row 3 of Lace Panel. Place sts onto waste yarn or st holder. Break yarn, leaving a 12" [30 cm] tail for finishing.

Finishing
Weave in ends. Block to measurements.
Sew shoulder edge of right and left fronts to back between shoulder placement markers.

Seam Neck Band
Transfer sts held for neck bands to 2 dpns. With RS together and using the three-needle bind off, BO all sts. Seam sides of band along back neck.

Bristol is a knitting teacher, designer, and finder-of-beauty-in-the-strangest-places from Portland, Maine. www.bristolivy.com Instagram: bristolivy

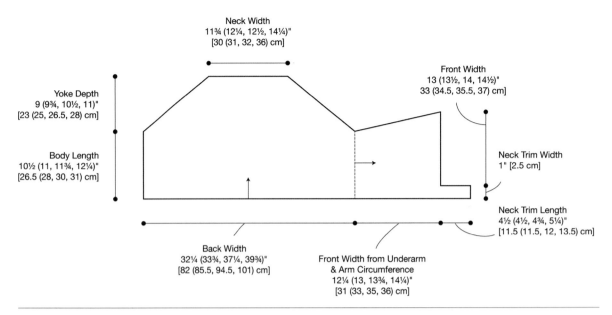

Neck Width
11¾ (12¼, 12½, 14¼)"
[30 (31, 32, 36) cm]

Front Width
13 (13½, 14, 14½)"
33 (34.5, 35.5, 37) cm]

Yoke Depth
9 (9¾, 10½, 11)"
[23 (25, 26.5, 28) cm]

Body Length
10½ (11, 11¾, 12¼)"
[26.5 (28, 30, 31) cm]

Neck Trim Width
1" [2.5 cm]

Neck Trim Length
4½ (4½, 4¾, 5¼)"
[11.5 (11.5, 12, 13.5) cm]

Back Width
32¼ (33¾, 37¼, 39¾)"
[82 (85.5, 94.5, 101) cm]

Front Width from Underarm
& Arm Circumference
12¼ (13, 13¾, 14¼)"
[31 (33, 35, 36) cm]

Open Waters Shawl
Melanie Berg

When I first started thinking about this design and what I wanted, I stumbled over a photograph of a whale shark and its fascinating patterning. I looked at many other pictures, but somehow kept coming back to this one. This shawl is my take on translating this graphic pattern into knitwear—its wavy lines, its dots and the fluid overall impression.

Canopy Fingering turned out to be the perfect yarn choice—its amazing stitch definition really lets the pattern shine.

Finished measurements
72" [183 cm] wingspan and 31" [78.5 cm] wide
Yarn
Canopy Fingering by The Fibre Company
(50% Alpaca, 30% Merino, 20% Bamboo; 50 grams / 200 yards [183 meters])

- 6 skeins in River Dolphin
OR
1100 yards [1005 meters] of fingering weight yarn
Needles
- One 40" [102 cm] circular needle (circ) in size US 2.5 [3 mm]
- One 24" [60 cm] circ or dpns in size US 5 [3.75 mm]
Or size to obtain gauge
Notions
- Stitch marker
- Tapestry needle
Gauge
23 sts and 44 rows = 4" [10 cm] in garter stitch with smaller needles, after blocking.

Special Abbreviations
dec 8 (decrease 8 sts): K2tog *k1, return 2 sts to LH needle, k2tog-tbl; rep from * six more times.
dec 9 (decrease 9 sts): K2tog *k1, return 2 sts to LH needle, k2tog-tbl; rep from * seven more times.
inc 5 (increase 5 sts): Insert LH needle from front to back under horizontal strand between st just worked and next st, then [k1, yo, k1, yo, k1] into this st.

Notes
Shawl is worked from narrow point on left edge, increasing to full side of right edge. Stitches are in-

creased every RS row to full width of stitch pattern, then new stitches are incorporated in garter stitch to end of shawl.

Shawl
With smaller circ and using the long-tail cast on, CO 3 sts. Do not join.
First row: (WS) Knit.

Begin border set up
Work Rows 1–38 of Set up Chart A—22 sts.
Work Rows 1–32 of Set up Chart B two times, then work Rows 1–31 one more time—79 sts.
Next row: (WS) K1, pm for border, *k3, p4, k3, p9; rep from * to last 2 sts, k2.

Set up garter stitch and border
Next row: (RS) K2, work Row 1 of Border Chart to m, sl m, k1-f/b (1 st inc'd)—80 sts.
Next row: Knit to m, sl m, work Border Chart to last 2 sts, k2.
Next row: K2, work Border Chart to m, sl m, knit to last st, k1-f/b (1 st inc'd at side edge).
Next row: Knit to m, sl m, work Border Chart to last 2 sts, k2.

Garter stitch and border
Note: All stitch counts account for 76 border stitches. If counting on a Row 3 or 11 of border, there will be 16 fewer stitches in border section.
Row 1: (RS) K2, work Border Chart to m, sl m, knit to last st, k1-f/b/f (2 sts inc'd)—83 sts.
Row 2 and all WS rows: Knit to m, sl m, work Border Chart to last 2 sts, k2.
Rows 3, 5, 7, and 9: K2, work Border Chart to m, knit to last st, k1-f/b (1 st inc'd)—87 sts.
Row 11: Rep Row 1—89 sts.
Rows 13, 15, 17, and 19: Rep Row 3—93 sts.
Row 21: Rep Row 1—95 sts.
Rows 23, 25, 27, 29, and 31: Rep Row 3—100 sts.
Row 32: Rep Row 2.
Rep Rows 1–32 eight more times, then work Rows 1–28 one more time—269 sts.
Next row: (RS) Work I-cord bind off as follows: With larger needle and the cable cast on, CO 3 sts, *k2, k2tog-tbl, return 3 sts to LH needle; rep from * to last 3 sts, k3tog-tbl. Cut yarn and draw through rem st.

Finishing
Weave in ends. Block to measurements.

Melanie is a knitwear designer who lives in Germany with her husband and three children.
www.mairlynd.wordpress.com Instagram: mairlynd

Set-up Chart A

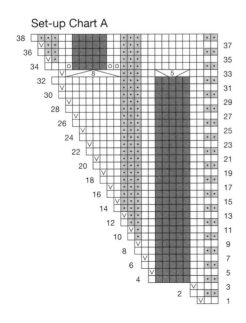

KEY

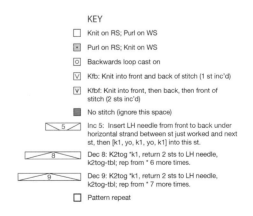

☐ Knit on RS; Purl on WS

• Purl on RS; Knit on WS

○ Backwards loop cast on

V Kfb: Knit into front and back of stitch (1 st inc'd)

V Kfbf: Knit into front, then back, then front of stitch (2 sts inc'd)

■ No stitch (ignore this space)

5 Inc 5: Insert LH needle from front to back under horizontal strand between st just worked and next st, then [k1, yo, k1, yo, k1] into this st.

8 Dec 8: K2tog *k1, return 2 sts to LH needle, k2tog-tbl; rep from * 6 more times.

9 Dec 9: K2tog *k1, return 2 sts to LH needle, k2tog-tbl; rep from * 7 more times.

☐ Pattern repeat

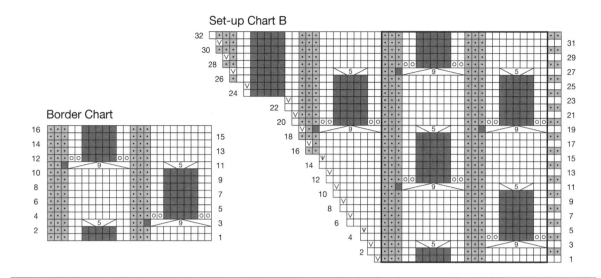

Set-up Chart B

Border Chart

Open Waters Cowl
Melanie Berg

This design is somewhat the little sister of my Open Waters Shawl. I was excited to try out the same stitch pattern with a much heavier weight yarn. As it turned out, Woolfolk's Tov was an equally great yarn choice! It has a wonderful stitch definition and an amazing softness. Looking at both designs, the shawl and the cowl, I find it pretty fascinating how different they are, but how similar at the same time.

Finished measurements
42" [106.5 cm] circumference and
10" [25.5 cm] deep

Yarn
TOV by Woolfolk
(100% Merino; 100 grams / 173 yards [158 meters])
• 3 skeins in T2
OR
430 yards [393 meters] of Aran weight yarn
Needles
• Two 24" [60 cm] circular needles in size US 7
  [4.5 mm]
Or size to obtain gauge
Notions
• Crochet hook and waste yarn for cast on
• Tapestry needle
Gauge
23 sts and 23 rows = 4" [10 cm] in stitch pattern, after blocking.

Special Abbreviations
dec 9 (decrease 9 sts): K2tog, *k1, return 2 sts to LH needle, k2tog-tbl; rep from * seven more times.
inc 5 (increase 5 sts): Insert LH needle from front to back under horizontal strand between st just worked and next st, then [k1, yo, k1, yo, k1] into this st.

Notes
Cowl is knit lengthwise, from a provisional cast on. Stitches from beginning and end are joined using the three-needle bind off.

Stitch pattern (multiple of 19 sts + 20)

(also, see chart below)

Row 1: (RS) K2, *k4, p3, k9, p3; rep from * one more time, k4, p3, k11.

Row 2: (WS) K2, p9, k3, p4, *k3, p9, k3, p4; rep from * one more time, k2.

Rows 3 and 4: Rep Rows 1 and 2.

Row 5: K2, *k2, inc 5, k2, p3, dec 9, p2; rep from * one more time, k2, inc 5, k2, p3, dec 9, k1 (12 sts dec'd).

Row 6: K2, bc 4, k3, p9, *k3, bc 4, k3, p9; rep from * one more time, k2 (12 sts inc'd).

Rows 7: K2, *k9, p3, k4, p3; rep from * one more time, k9, p3, k6.

Row 8: K2, p4, k3, p9, *k3, p4, k3, p9; rep from * one more time, k2.

Rows 9-12: Rep Rows 7 and 8 two times.

Row 13: K2, *dec 9, p2, k2, inc 5, k2, p3; rep from * one more time, dec 9, p2, k2, inc 5, k4 (12 sts dec'd).

Row 14: K2, p9, k3, bc 4, *k3, p9, k3, bc 4; rep from * one more time, k2 (12 sts inc'd).

Rows 15 and 16: Rep Rows 1 and 2.

Cowl

Using the crochet provisional cast on, CO 58 sts. Do not join.

First row: (WS) K2, *p9, k3, p4, k3; rep from * one more time, p9, k3, p4, k2.

Begin stitch pattern

Work Rows 1–16 of Cowl Chart a total of 15 times.

Join cowl ends

Carefully unzip the provisional cast on and place 58 sts onto second circ. With RS together and using the three-needle bind off, BO all sts.

Finishing

Weave in ends. Block cowl to measurements.

Cowl Chart

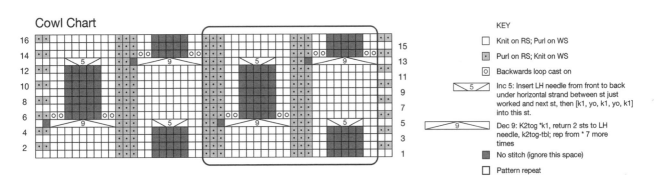

KEY

- ☐ Knit on RS; Purl on WS
- ▪ Purl on RS; Knit on WS
- ○ Backwards loop cast on
- ⟍5⟋ Inc 5: Insert LH needle from front to back under horizontal strand between st just worked and next st, then [k1, yo, k1, yo, k1] into this st.
- ⟍9⟋ Dec 9: K2tog *k1, return 2 sts to LH needle, k2tog-tbl; rep from * 7 more times
- ■ No stitch (ignore this space)
- ☐ Pattern repeat

Arctic Cardigan
Carrie Bostick Hoge

Arctic Cardigan is inspired by the thick coats of fur found on fauna living in the arctic. The stitches are left simple (mainly stockinette) so the yarn can easily display its rustic texture, which conjurs thoughts of animals' fleece in winter.

Finished measurements
31 (33¼, 36½, 40, 43½, 47, 50¼, 53¾, 57¼)" [78.5 (84.5, 92.5, 101.5, 110.5, 119.5, 127.5, 136.5, 145.5) cm] bust circumference, buttoned; sample shown in size 33¼" with -¾" [2 cm] ease. Suggested Ease -1 to 3" [-2.5 to 7.5 cm]

Yarn
Quarry by Brooklyn Tweed
(100% wool; 100 grams / 200 yards [182 meters])
• 5 (5, 6, 6, 6, 7, 7, 8, 8) skeins in Moonstone
OR
842 (913, 1008, 1120, 1187, 1272, 1355, 1440, 1575) yards [770 (835, 922, 1024, 1085, 1163, 1239, 1317, 1440) meters] in chunky weight yarn

Needles
• One 16" and 32" circular (circ) each in size US 10.5 [6.5 mm]
• One pair straight in size US 10.5 [6.5 mm]
Or size to obtain gauge

Notions
• Stitch markers (m)
• Stitch holders or waste yarn
• Tapestry needle
• Seven ¾" [2 cm] buttons

Gauge
14 sts and 21 rows = 4" [10 cm] in stockinette stitch, after blocking.

Notes
Cardigan is worked from the top down.

Circular needle is used to accommodate large number of stitches.

Work all slipped stitches with yarn in back as if to knit.

It is suggested to use different colored markers for the bands than for the raglan, sides and pockets, to easily tell them apart.

Cardigan
Collar
Note: Change to longer circ when sts no longer fit comfortably on shorter circ.
With shorter circ and using the long-tail cast on, CO 56 (56, 64, 64, 64, 68, 68, 68, 72) sts. Do not join.

Begin Collar
First row: (WS) Sl 1 with yarn in back as if to knit, k6, [p2, k2] to last 9 sts, p2, k7.
Next row: (RS) Sl 1 with yarn in back as if to knit, k6, [k2, p2] to last 9 sts, k9.
Rep last 2 rows until collar meas 3" [7.5 cm] from CO edge, ending after a RS row.

Yoke
Begin garter stitch bands and St st yoke
First row *place markers:* (WS) Sl 1, k6 for band, pm for band, p7 (7, 8, 8, 8, 9, 9, 9, 10) for Right Front, pm for raglan, p4 (4, 6, 6, 6, 6, 6, 6, 6) for Sleeve, pm for raglan, p20 (20, 22, 22, 22, 24, 24, 24, 26) for Back, pm for raglan, p4 (4, 6, 6, 6, 6, 6, 6, 6) for Sleeve, pm for raglan, p7 (7, 8, 8, 8, 9, 9, 9, 10) for Left Front, pm for band, k7 for band.

Begin raglan shaping
Note: Read the following instructions carefully before beginning: Buttonholes begin 1" [2.5 cm] into the raglan shaping, and are worked *at the same time* as the yoke and continue through the body.
Next row *inc row:* (RS) Knit to 1 st before raglan marker, k1/R, sl m, k1, k1/R; rep from * three more times, work to end as est (8 sts inc'd)—64 (64, 72, 72, 72, 76, 76, 76, 80) sts.
Work 1 WS row even as est, keeping band sts in garter st and all other sts in St st.

Rep *inc row* every other row 14 (15, 16, 17, 17, 19, 21, 22, 23) times—176 (184, 200, 208, 208, 228, 244, 252, 264) sts; 29 (30, 32, 33, 33, 36, 38, 39, 40) sts each front, 34 (36, 40, 42, 42, 46, 50, 52, 54) sts each sleeve and 50 (52, 56, 58, 58, 64, 68, 70, 74) sts for back; AND AT THE SAME TIME: **Begin Buttonholes**, when yoke meas 1" [2.5 cm] (or 4" [10 cm] from CO edge), ending after a WS row.

Buttonhole Row 1: (RS) Work as est to last band m, sl m, k1, k2tog, [yo] two times, k2tog, k2.

Buttonhole Row 2: (WS) Work as est to buttonhole, knit into yo, knit into back of extra wrap, knit to end.

Work 12 rows as est.

Rep Buttonhole Rows 1 and 2.

Rep last 14 rows 5 (5, 5, 6, 6, 6, 6, 6, 7) more times (7 (7, 7, 8, 8, 8, 8, 8, 9) buttonholes total).

Continue raglan shaping

For sizes 31 (33¼, -, -, -, -, -, -, -)" only
Skip to All Sizes below.

For sizes - (-, 36½, 40, 43½, 47, 50¼, 53¾, 57¼)"
Inc the body only on every row - (-, 1, 3, 5, 5, 6, 7, 8) times, working the inc rows as follows:

Next row *body only inc row:* (WS) *Work to 1 st before raglan m, p1/R, sl m, work to next m, sl m, p1, p1/R; rep from * one more time, work to end (4 sts inc'd).

Next row *body only inc row:* (RS) *Work to 1 st before raglan m, k1/R, sl m, work to next m, sl m, k1, k1/R; rep from * one more time, work to end (4 sts inc'd).

All Sizes

When all raglan shaping is complete there are 176 (184, 204, 220, 228, 248, 268, 280, 296) sts; 29 (30, 33, 36, 38, 41, 44, 46, 49) sts each front, 34 (36, 40, 42, 42, 46, 50, 52, 54) sts each sleeve and 50 (52, 58, 64, 68, 74, 80, 84, 90) sts for back.

If necessary, work 1 WS row even to end after a WS row.

Next row: (RS) Work as est to first raglan m, remove m, sl next 34 (36, 40, 42, 42, 46, 50, 52, 54) sleeve sts to st holder or waste yarn, remove m, using the backward loop cast on, CO 2 (3, 3, 3, 4, 4, 4, 5, 5) sts, pm for side, CO 2 (3, 3, 3, 4, 4, 4, 5, 5) more sts, work across back sts to next raglan m, remove m, slip next sleeve 34 (36, 40, 42, 42, 46, 50, 52, 54) sts to st holder or waste yarn, remove m, using the backward loop cast on, CO 2 (3, 3, 3, 4, 4, 4, 5, 5) sts, pm for side, CO 2 (3, 3, 3, 4, 4, 4, 5, 5) more sts, work as est to end— 116 (124, 136, 148, 160, 172, 184, 196, 208) body sts rem on needle.

Body

Cont to work bands as est and all other sts in St st until body meas 2" [5 cm] from underarm, ending after a WS row.

Begin side shaping

Next row *inc row:* (RS) Work band as est, sl m, *knit to 2 sts before side m, m1-R, k2, sl m, k2, m1-L; rep from * one more time, work as est to end (4 sts inc'd)—120 (128, 140, 152, 164, 176, 188, 200, 212) sts.

Rep *inc row* every 12th row two more times—128 (136, 148, 160, 172, 184, 196, 208, 220) sts. Remove side markers.

Cont to work bands as est and all other sts in St st until body meas 11 (11, 11, 11.5, 11.5, 11, 10, 10, 11)" [28 (28, 28, 29, 29, 28, 25.5, 25.5, 28) cm] from underarm, ending after a WS row.

Begin hem pocket

Next row: (RS) Work as est to band m, sl m, k2, p2, transfer next 18 sts onto st holder or waste yarn for pocket lining, using the backward loop cast on, CO 18 sts, *p2, k2; rep from * to last 31 sts, p2, transfer next 18 sts onto st holder or waste yarn for pocket lining, using the backward loop cast on, CO 18 sts, p2, k2, sl m, work band as est to end.

Next row: (WS) Work as est to band m, sl m, *p2, k2; rep from * to last 9 sts, p2, sl m, work band as est to end.

Next row: (RS) Work as est to band m, sl m, [k2, p2] to last 9 sts, k2, sl m, work band as est to end. Rep last 2 rows until hem meas 5" [12.5 cm] from beg of 2x2 ribbing, ending after a WS row.

Next row: (RS) Loosely BO all sts in pattern.

Sleeves

Transfer 34 (36, 40, 42, 42, 46, 50, 52, 54) held sts from one sleeve to shorter circ. Do not join. Note: Change to straight needles when comfortable, if desired.

Next row: (WS) Using the backward loop cast on, CO 2 (3, 3, 3, 4, 4, 4, 5, 5) sts, knit to end, CO another 2 (3, 3, 3, 4, 4, 4, 5, 5) sts—38 (42, 46, 48, 50, 54, 58, 62, 64) sts.

Cont in St st until sleeve meas 2 (2, 1, 1, 1, 1, 1, 1, 1)" [5 (5, 2.5, 2.5, 2.5, 2.5, 2.5, 2.5, 2.5) cm] from underarm, ending after a WS row.

Begin sleeve shaping

Next row *dec row:* (RS) K2, k2tog, knit to last 4 sts, ssk, k2 (2 sts dec'd)—36 (40, 44, 46, 48, 52, 56, 60, 62) sts rem.
Rep *dec row* every 16 (16, 12, 14, 12, 8, 8, 8, 6) rows 3 (3, 3, 4, 3, 7, 7, 1, 8) times, then every 0 (0, 10, 0, 10, 0, 0, 6, 4) rows 0 (0, 2, 0, 2, 0, 0, 8, 2) times—30 (34, 34, 38, 38, 38, 42, 42, 42) sts rem.

Cont even in St st until sleeve meas 14" [35.5 cm] from underarm, ending after a WS row.

Begin 2x2 rib

Next row: (RS) K1, *k2, p2; rep from * to last st, k1.
Next row: (WS) P1, *k2, p2; rep from * to last st, p1.
Rep last 2 rows until cuff meas 4½" [11.5 cm], ending after a WS row.

Next row: (RS) BO all sts in pattern.
Work second sleeve the same as the first.

Pocket linings

Transfer 18 held sts from one pocket to larger straight needle ready to work a RS row.
Next row: (RS) Using the backward loop cast on, CO 1 st, knit to end, CO 1 more st—20 sts.
Cont in St st for 5" [12.5 cm], ending after a WS row.

Next row: (RS) BO all sts knitwise.
Work second pocket lining the same as the first.

Finishing

Steam- or wet-block to measurements. Sew pocket linings to inside of sweater. Sew sleeves and underarms. Sew buttons opposite buttonholes.

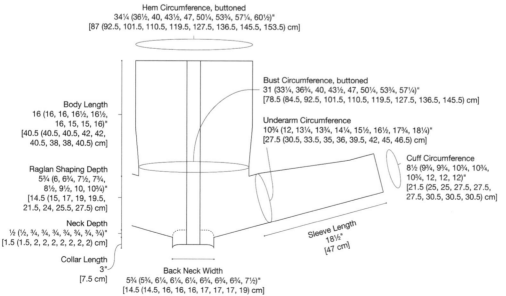

Hem Circumference, buttoned
34¼ (36½, 40, 43½, 47, 50¼, 53¾, 57¼, 60½)"
[87 (92.5, 101.5, 110.5, 119.5, 127.5, 136.5, 145.5, 153.5) cm]

Bust Circumference, buttoned
31 (33¼, 36¾, 40, 43½, 47, 50¼, 53¾, 57¼)"
[78.5 (84.5, 92.5, 101.5, 110.5, 119.5, 127.5, 136.5, 145.5) cm]

Underarm Circumference
10¾ (12, 13¼, 13¾, 14¼, 15½, 16½, 17¾, 18¼)"
[27.5 (30.5, 33.5, 35, 36, 39.5, 42, 45, 46.5) cm]

Body Length
16 (16, 16, 16½, 16½, 16, 15, 15, 16)"
[40.5 (40.5, 40.5, 42, 42, 40.5, 38, 38, 40.5) cm]

Raglan Shaping Depth
5¾ (6, 6¾, 7½, 7¾, 8½, 9½, 10, 10¾)"
[14.5 (15, 17, 19, 19.5, 21.5, 24, 25.5, 27.5) cm]

Neck Depth
½ (½, ¾, ¾, ¾, ¾, ¾, ¾, ¾)"
[1.5 (1.5, 2, 2, 2, 2, 2, 2, 2) cm]

Collar Length
3"
[7.5 cm]

Cuff Circumference
8½ (9¾, 9¾, 10¾, 10¾, 10¾, 12, 12, 12)"
[21.5 (25, 25, 27.5, 27.5, 27.5, 30.5, 30.5, 30.5) cm]

Sleeve Length
18½"
[47 cm]

Back Neck Width
5¾ (5¾, 6¼, 6¼, 6¼, 6¾, 6¾, 6¾, 7½)"
[14.5 (14.5, 16, 16, 16, 17, 17, 17, 19) cm]

Arctic Cowl
Carrie Bostick Hoge

This cowl, same as the Arctic Cardigan, is inspired by the many layers of faunas' fur and feathers needed to stay warm in the cold arctic climate. Arctic cowl is worked in St. Magnus DK yarn, which has the warm halo effect from the angora.

Finished measurements
20" [51 cm] circumference and 8" [20.5 cm] deep

Yarn
St Magnus DK by Orkney Angora
(50% angora, 50% lambswool; 50 grams / 218 yards [199 meters]
• 1 skein in Ghost (color exclusive to Loop, London)
OR
185 yards [169 meters] of DK weight yarn

Needles
• One 16" [40 cm] circular needle (circ) in size US 5 [3.75 mm]
Or size to obtain gauge

Notions
• Stitch marker
• Tapestry needle

Gauge
26 sts and 8 rnds = 4" [10 cm] in Arctic stitch pattern, after blocking.

Cowl
Using the long-tail cast on, CO 130 sts. Place marker for BOR, being careful not to twist sts.

Begin Arctic stitch pattern (multiple of 26 sts)
Rnd 1 and all odd-numbered rnds: Knit.
Rnd 2: *K1, m1, ssk, k4, k2tog, k3, m1, k2, m1, k3, ssk, k4, k2tog, m1, k1; rep from * to end.
Rnd 4: *K1, m1, k1, ssk, k2, k2tog, k4, m1, k2, m1, k4, ssk, k2, k2tog, k1, m1, k1; rep from * to end.
Rnd 6: *K1, m1, k2, ssk, k2tog, k5, m1, k2, m1, k5, ssk, k2tog, k2, m1, k1; rep from * to end.
Rnd 8: *K1, m1, k3, ssk, k4, k2tog, m1, k2, m1, ssk, k4, k2tog, k3, m1, k1; rep from * to end.
Rnd 10: *K1, m1, k4, ssk, k2, k2tog, k1, m1, k2, m1, k1, ssk, k2, k2tog, k4, m1, k1; rep from * to end.
Rnd 12: *K1, m1, k5, ssk, k2tog, k2, [m1, k2] two times, ssk, k2tog, k5, m1, k1; rep from * to end.
Work Rnds 1–12 of Arctic stitch pattern until cowl meas approx 8" [20.5 cm] from beg, ending after Rnd 12 of stitch pattern.
Next rnd *dec rnd:* K11, k2tog; rep from * to end (10 sts dec'd)—120 sts rem.
Next rnd: BO all sts knitwise.

Finishing
Weave in ends. Wet-block to measurements.

Wild Feather Mitts
Cecily Glowik MacDonald

Wild Turkeys are a frequent sight here in Maine. They cross the street and wander through fields. And if you take a walk through the woods, chances are you might find one of their incredible feathers.

Finished measurements
7¾" [19.5cm] palm circumference and 6½" [16.5cm] length

Yarn

Pioneer by A Verb for Keeping Warm
(100% organic merino; 50 grams / 160 yards
[146 meters])
• 1 skein Grizzly Peak
OR 130 yards [119 meters] in a light worsted
weight yarn

Needles

• One set double-pointed needles (dpns) in size
  US 5 [3.75 mm]
Or size to obtain gauge

Notions

• Stitch markers
• Stitch holders or waste yarn
• Tapestry needle

Gauge

20 sts and 30 rnds = 4" [10 cm] in stockinette
stitch, after blocking.

Wild Feather Panel (also, see chart)

Rnd 1: P2, k2, p1, k1, p1, k2, p2.
Rnd 2: P1, k2, p2, k1, p2, k2, p1.
Rnd 3: K2, p2, k3, p2, k2.
Rnd 4: K1, p2, k5, p2, k1.
Rep Rnds 1–4 for Wild Feather Panel.

Left Mitt

With dpns and using the long-tail cast on, CO 34
sts. Place marker (pm) and join to begin working in
the rnd, being careful not to twist sts.
First rnd: *K1, p1; rep from * to end.
Rep the last rnd until pc meas 2½" [6.5 cm] from
cast on edge.

Begin Wild Feather Panel

Next rnd *inc rnd:* (K1-f/b) two times, k9, work
next 11 sts in Wild Feather Panel, k11, k1-f/b
(3 sts inc'd)—37 sts.

Begin Thumb Gusset

Next rnd *set-up rnd:* K8, pm, k1-f/b/f, pm, work
to end as est in Wild Feather Panel and St st (2
gusset sts inc'd)—39 sts; 3 sts between markers.

Shape Gusset

Work 1 rnd even as est in Wild Feather Panel and
St st.
Next rnd *inc rnd:* Work to m as est, sl m,
k1/R, work to 1 st before m, k1/R, sl m, work

to end as est (2 gusset sts inc'd)—41 sts; 5 sts
between markers.
Rep the last 2 rnds five more times—51 sts; 15 sts
between markers.

Work 1 rnd even.

Separate for Thumb and Hand

Next rnd: Work to m as est, remove m, place
next 14 sts onto st holder or waste yarn, using the
backward loop cast on, CO 2 sts, k1, remove m,
knit to end—39 sts rem.
Work even as est until pc meas 1½" [4 cm] from
separation of thumb and hand.

Next rnd: *K1, p1; rep from * to last st, k1.
Rep the last rnd two more times.
Next rnd: BO all sts in rib.

Right Mitt

Work the same as the Left Mitt to the beg of
thumb gusset.
Next rnd *set-up rnd:* Work as est in Wild Feather
Panel and St st to last 9 sts, pm, k1-f/b/f, pm, knit
to end (2 sts inc'd)—39 sts.
Cont working the same as the Left Mitt.

Thumb

Place 14 held thumb gusset sts onto dpn, pick up
and knit 2 sts in CO sts in hand and join to work in
the rnd—16 sts.
Knit 1 rnd.
Next rnd: *K1, p1; rep from * to end.
Rep the last rnd two more times.

Next rnd: BO all sts in rib.
Rep for second mitt.

Finishing

Weave in ends.
Block to measurements.

*Cecily is a knitwear designer in
Portland, ME.
www.cecilyam.wordpress.com
Instagram: cecilyam*

Wild Feather Panel

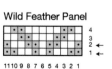

11 10 9 8 7 6 5 4 3 2 1

KEY

☐ Knit on RS; Purl on WS
⊡ Purl on RS; Knit on WS

Stag Head Pullover
Norah Gaughan

When Carrie mentioned that the theme of this issue would be Fauna I immediately knew I wanted to draw with cables. Remembering an inspirational cabled skull pullover by Alexander McQueen I set out to emulate the feeling with a stag's head and his wonderful rack of antlers.

Finished measurements
36½ (40, 43½, 47, 50¾, 54¼, 57¾, 61¼)" [92.5 (101.5, 110.5, 119.5, 129, 138, 146.5, 155.5) cm] bust circumference; sample shown in size 40" [101.5 cm] with 6" [15 cm] positive ease
Suggested ease: 4" [10 cm] to 6" [15 cm] positive ease

Yarn
Erin by Imperial Yarn Co.
(100% wool; 4 oz / 225 yards [206 meters])
• 5 (5, 6, 6, 7, 7, 7, 8) skeins in Rain
OR
1045 (1120, 1245, 1310, 1465, 1520, 1640, 1715) yards [959 (1027, 1140, 1200, 1343, 1391, 1503, 1568) meters] in light worsted weight yarn

Needles
• One pair each in sizes US 5 and 7 [3.75 and 4.5 mm]
• One 16" [40 cm] circular needle (circ) in size US 5 [3.75 mm]
Or size to obtain gauge

Notions
• Stitch markers
• Cable needle
• Tapestry needle

Gauge
18 sts and 26 rows = 4" [10 cm] in stockinette stitch with larger needles, after blocking.
Body panel = 16" [40.5 cm], after blocking.

Notes
Pullover is worked in pieces, then seamed together. Stitches are picked up around neck for rib trim.

Back
Using smaller needles and the alternating cable cast on, CO 122 (130, 138, 146, 158, 166, 174, 182) sts.
Row 1: (RS) *K2, p2, rep from * to last 2 sts, k2.
Row 2: (WS) *P2, k2, rep from * to last 2 sts, p2.
Cont in rib for 2½" [6.5 cm], ending after a RS row. Change to larger needles.
Next row *dec row:* (WS) Purl to end and using p2tog, decrease 12 (12, 12, 12, 16, 16, 16, 16) sts evenly across row—110 (118, 126, 134, 142, 150, 158, 166) sts rem.

Begin stitch patterns
Next row: (RS) K12 (16, 20, 24, 28, 32, 36, 40), pm, work Row 1 of Body Panel over 86 sts, pm, k12 (16, 20, 24, 28, 32, 36, 40).
Cont in St st and Body Panel for 17 (15, 19, 15, 21, 17, 21, 19) more rows.

Begin side shaping
Next row *dec row:* (RS) K2, k2tog, cont to work in St st and Body Panel to last 4 sts, ssk, k2 (2 sts dec'd)—108 (116, 124, 132, 140, 148, 156, 164) sts rem.
Rep *dec row* every 8 rows six more times—96 (104, 112, 120, 128, 136, 144, 152) sts rem.
Work 19 rows even.
Pc meas approx 15¾ (15½, 16, 15½, 16¼, 15¾, 16¼, 16)" [40 (39.5, 40.5, 39.5, 41.5, 40, 41.5, 40.5) cm] from beg.

Begin armhole shaping
Next row: (RS) BO 2 (3, 3, 4, 4, 4, 5, 5) sts, work to end—94 (101, 109, 116, 124, 132, 139, 147) sts rem.
Next row: (WS) BO 2 (3, 3, 4, 4, 4, 5, 5) sts, work to end—92 (98, 106, 112, 120, 128, 134, 142) sts rem.
Next row: BO 2 (2, 3, 3, 4, 5, 5, 6) sts, work to end—90 (96, 103, 109, 116, 123, 129, 136) sts rem.
Next row: BO 2 (2, 3, 3, 4, 5, 5, 6) sts, work to end—88 (94, 100, 106, 112, 118, 124, 130) sts rem.

Next row *dec row:* (RS) K1, k2tog, work to last 3 sts, ssk, k1 (2 sts dec'd)—86 (92, 98, 104, 110, 116, 122, 128) sts.

Rep *dec row* every RS row 2 (3, 3, 3, 5, 6, 8, 9) more times—82 (86, 92, 98, 100, 104, 106, 110) sts rem.

Next row: (WS) P1, k1, work as est to last 2 sts, k1, p1.

Next row: K1, p1, work to last 2 sts, p1, k1.

Cont as est until pc meas 7 (7½, 8, 8½, 9, 9½, 10, 10½)" [18 (19, 20.5, 21.5, 23, 24, 25.5, 26.5) cm] from underarm, ending after a WS row.

Begin shoulder and neck shaping

Mark center 26 sts.

Next row: (RS) BO 4 sts, work to end—78 (82, 88, 94, 96, 100, 102, 106) sts rem.

Next row: (WS) BO 4 sts, work to end—74 (78, 84, 90, 92, 96, 98, 102) sts rem.

Rep the last 2 rows one more time—66 (70, 76, 82, 84, 88, 90, 94) sts rem.

Next row: (RS) BO 4 (4, 5, 6, 6, 6, 6, 7) sts, work to m, join a new ball of yarn and BO center 26 sts, work to end—20 (22, 25, 28, 29, 31, 32, 34) sts rem for left shoulder, 16 (18, 20, 22, 23, 25, 26, 27) sts for right.

Next row: (WS) BO 4 (4, 5, 6, 6, 6, 6, 7) sts, work to neck; then BO 5 (5, 5, 5, 5, 6, 6, 6) sts, work to end—16 (18, 20, 22, 23, 25, 26, 27) sts left shoulder, 11 (13, 15, 17, 18, 19, 20, 21) sts for right.

Next row: BO 4 (4, 5, 6, 6, 6, 7, 7) sts, work to neck; then BO 5 (5, 5, 5, 5, 6, 6, 6) sts, work to end—11 (13, 15, 17, 18, 19, 20, 21) sts for left shoulder, 7 (9, 10, 11, 12, 13, 13, 14) sts for right.

Next row: BO 4 (4, 5, 6, 6, 6, 7, 7) sts, work to neck; then BO 4 (5, 5, 5, 5, 6, 6, 7) sts, work to end—7 (9, 10, 11, 12, 13, 13, 14) sts for left shoulder, 3 (4, 5, 6, 7, 7, 7, 7) sts for right.

Next row: (RS) BO rem right sts; then BO 4 (5, 5, 5, 5, 6, 6, 7) sts, work to end—3 (4, 5, 6, 6, 7, 7, 7) sts for left shoulder.

Next row: (WS) BO rem sts.

Front

Work Front same as for Back through armhole shaping, except once you have worked Rows 1–8 of Body Panel a total of 4 (4, 5, 5, 6, 6, 7, 7) times, begin with Row 1 of Stag Panel and cont in Stag Panel for remainder of Front. Note varying stitch counts in Stag Panel and account for this when counting stitches on shaping rows.

Last row worked in body before underarm will be Row 54 (52, 48, 44, 42, 38, 34, 32) of Stag Panel. Once you reach Row 87 of Stag Panel, there will be 78 (82, 88, 94, 96, 100, 102, 106) sts on needle. Begin neck shaping on the following WS row.

Begin neck shaping

Mark center 16 (18, 18, 18, 18, 22, 22, 24) sts for neck.

Next row: (WS) Work to neck m, join a new ball of yarn and BO center 16 (18, 18, 18, 18, 22, 22, 24) sts, work to end—31 (32, 35, 38, 39, 39, 40, 41) sts rem for each shoulder. Cont working chart over rem sts.

Next row: (RS) Work to neck; then BO 4 sts, work to end.

Next row: Work to neck; then BO 4 sts, work to end—27 (28, 31, 34, 35, 35, 36, 37) sts rem for each shoulder.

Next row: (RS) Work to neck; then BO 3 sts, work to end.

Next row: Work to neck; then BO 3 sts, work to end—24 (25, 28, 31, 32, 32, 33, 34) sts each.

Next row: (RS) Work to neck; then BO 2 sts, work to end.

Next row: Work to neck; then BO 2 sts, work to end—22 (23, 26, 29, 30, 30, 31, 32) sts each.

Next row: (RS) Work to neck; then BO 1 st, work to end.

Next row: Work to neck; then BO 1 st, work to end—21 (22, 25, 28, 29, 29, 30, 31) sts each.

Rep the last 2 rows three more times—18 (19, 22, 25, 26, 26, 27, 28) sts rem for each shoulder.

Work even until front meas same as back at armhole edge, ending after a WS row.

Begin shoulder shaping

Next row: (RS) BO 4 sts, work to neck; then work to end.

Next row: (WS) BO 4 sts, work to neck; then work to end—14 (15, 18, 21, 22, 22, 23, 24) sts rem for each shoulder.

Rep the last 2 rows one more time—10 (11, 14, 17, 18, 18, 19, 20) sts rem for each shoulder.

Next row: (RS) BO 4 (4, 5, 6, 6, 6, 6, 7) sts, work to neck; then work to end.

Next row: BO 4 (4, 5, 6, 6, 6, 6, 7) sts, work to neck; then work to end—6 (7, 9, 11, 12, 12, 13, 13) sts rem for each shoulder.

Next row: (RS) BO 4 (4, 5, 6, 6, 6, 7, 7) sts, work to neck; then work to end.

Next row: BO 4 (4, 5, 6, 6, 6, 7, 7) sts, work to neck; then work to end—2 (3, 4, 5, 6, 6, 6, 6) sts rem for each shoulder.

Next row: (RS) BO rem sts to neck; then work to end.

Next row: BO rem sts.

Sleeves (make 2)

Using smaller needles and the alternating cable cast on, CO 40 (40, 44, 44, 48, 48, 52, 52) sts. Do not join.

Row 1: (RS) *K2, p2, rep from * to last 2 sts, k2.
Row 2: (WS) *P2, k2, rep from * to last 2 sts, p2.
Cont in rib for 2" [5 cm], ending after a RS row. Change to larger needles.

Next row dec row: (WS) Purl to end and using p2tog, dec 4 (4, 6, 6, 6, 6, 8, 8) sts evenly across row—36 (36, 38, 38, 42, 42, 44, 44) sts rem.

Begin stitch patterns

Next row: (RS) K3 (3, 4, 4, 6, 6, 7, 7), pm, work Row 1 of Sleeve Panel over 30 sts, pm, k3 (3, 4, 4, 6, 6, 7, 7).
Cont in St st and sleeve panel for 9 (9, 5, 5, 3, 1, 1, 1) more rows.

Begin sleeve shaping

Next row inc row: (RS) K2, m1-L, work to last 2 sts, m1-R, k2 (2 sts inc'd)—38 (38, 40, 40, 44, 44, 46, 46) sts.
Rep *inc row* every 12 (10, 8, 6, 6, 4, 4, 4) rows 2 (8, 8, 6, 13, 1, 4, 7) more times, then every 14 (0, 10, 8, 8, 6, 6, 6) rows 4 (0, 2, 6, 1, 14, 12, 10) times—50 (54, 60, 64, 72, 74, 78, 80) sts on needle.
Work even until pc meas 17" [43 cm] from beg, ending after a WS row.

Begin cap shaping

Next row: (RS) BO 2 (3, 3, 4, 4, 4, 5, 5) sts, work to end—48 (51, 57, 60, 68, 70, 73, 75) sts rem.

Next row: (WS) BO 2 (3, 3, 4, 4, 4, 5, 5) sts, work to end—46 (48, 54, 56, 64, 66, 68, 70) sts rem.
Next row: BO 2 (2, 3, 3, 4, 5, 5, 6) sts, work to end—44 (46, 51, 53, 60, 61, 63, 64) sts rem.
Next row: BO 2 (2, 3, 3, 4, 5, 5, 6) sts, work to end—42 (44, 48, 50, 56, 56, 58, 58) sts rem.
Next row dec row: (RS) K1, k2tog, work to last 3 sts, ssk, k1 (2 sts dec'd)—40 (42, 46, 48, 54, 54, 56, 56) sts.
Rep *dec row* every RS row 3 (3, 3, 5, 5, 5, 5) more times, every 4 rows 2 (2, 2, 2, 0, 0, 0, 0) times, then every RS row 3 (3, 3, 3, 6, 6, 6, 6)—24 (26, 30, 32, 32, 32, 34, 34) sts.
Next row: (RS) BO 2 sts, work to end—22 (24, 28, 30, 30, 30, 32, 32) sts.
Next row: (WS) BO 2 sts, work to end—20 (22, 26, 28, 28, 28, 30, 30) sts.
Next row: BO 3 sts, work to end—17 (19, 23, 25, 25, 25, 27, 27) sts.
Next row: BO 3 sts, work to end—14 (16, 20, 22, 22, 22, 24, 24) sts rem.
Next row: BO rem sts.

Finishing

Weave in ends. Block to measurements
Sew shoulder seams. (Note that front shoulders contain 1 fewer stitch than back.)
Set in sleeves, then seam sides and sleeves.

Neck trim

With smaller circ and RS facing, beg at center of back neck, pick up and knit 90 (92, 92, 92, 92, 96, 96, 98) sts around neck opening.
Pm for BOR.
Next rnd: *K1, p1; rep from * to end.
Cont in rib for 1¼" [3 cm].
Next rnd: Using the tubular bind off (or your preferred stretchy bind off), BO all sts.

Norah is a knitwear designer and author of Knitted Cable Sourcebook, *living in New Hampshire.*
www.norahgaughan.net Instagram: norahgn

Stag Head Pullover

KEY

- ☐ Knit on RS; Purl on WS
- ⊡ Purl on RS; Knit on WS
- ▓ no stitch (ignore this space)
- ▣ p2tog (1 st dec'd)
- ▣ k-tbl: knit 1 through the back loop
- 2/2 RT: Sl 2 to CN, hold to back, k2, k2 from CN
- 2/2 LT: Sl 2 to CN, hold to front, k2, k2 from CN
- 2/1 RT: Sl 1 to CN, hold to back, k2, k1 from CN
- 2/1 LT: Sl 2 to CN, hold to front, k1, k2 from CN
- 1/1 RC: Sl 1 to CN, hold to back, k1, p1 from CN
- 1/1 LC: Sl 1 to CN, hold to front, p1, k1 from CN
- 1/1 RT: Sl 1 to CN, hold to back, k1, k1 from CN
- 1/1 LT: Sl 1 to CN, hold to front, k1, k1 from CN
- 2/2 RC: Sl 2 to CN, hold to back, k2, p2 from CN
- 2/2 LC: Sl 2 to CN, hold to front, p2, k2 from CN
- 1/2 RC: Sl 2 to CN, hold to back, k1, p2 from CN
- 1/2 LC: Sl 1 to CN, hold to front, p2, k1 from CN
- 2/1 RC: Sl 1 to CN, hold to back, k2, p1 from CN
- 2/1 LC: Sl 2 to CN, hold to front, p1, k2 from CN
- 1/2 RT: Sl 2 to CN, hold to back, k1, k2 from CN
- 1/2 LT: Sl 1 to CN, hold to front, k2, k1 from CN

- 2/3 RT: Sl 3 to CN, hold to back, k2, k3 from CN
- 2/3 LT: Sl 2 to CN, hold to front, k3, k2 from CN
- 3/1 RT: Sl 1 to CN, hold to back, k3, k1 from CN
- 3/1 LT: Sl 3 to CN, hold to front, k1, k3 from CN
- 3/1 RC: Sl 1 to CN, hold to back, k3, p1 from CN
- 3/1 LC: Sl 3 to CN, hold to front, p1, k3 from CN
- 3/2 RC: Sl 2 to CN, hold to back, k3, p2 from CN
- 3/2 LC: Sl 3 to CN, hold to front, p2, k3 from CN
- 4/1 RC: Sl 1 to CN, hold to back, k4, p1 from CN
- 4/1 LC: Sl 4 to CN, hold to front, p1, k4 from CN
- 4/2 RC: Sl 2 to CN, hold to back, k4, p2 from CN
- 4/2 LC: Sl 4 to CN, hold to front, p2, k4 from CN
- 4/2 RC-dec: Sl 2 to CN, hold to back, k4, p2tog from CN (1 st dec'd)
- 4/2 LC-dec: Sl 4 to CN, hold to front, p2tog, k4 from CN (1 st dec'd)
- 4/3 RT: Sl 3 to CN, hold to back, k4, k3 from CN
- 4/3 LT: Sl 4 to CN, hold to front, k3, k4 from CN
- 4/3 RC: Sl 3 to CN, hold to back, k4, p3 from CN
- 4/3 LC: Sl 4 to CN, hold to front, p3, k4 from CN
- 2/2 RT-inc: Sl 2 to CN, hold to back, k2, (k1, yo, k1) from CN (1 st inc'd)
- 2/2 LT-inc: Sl 2 to CN, hold to front, (k1, yo, k1), k2 from CN (1 st inc'd)
- 4/2 RT-inc: Sl 2 to CN, hold to back, k4, (yo, k1, yo, k1) from CN (2 sts inc'd)
- 4/2 LT-inc: Sl 4 to CN, hold to front, (k1, yo, k1, yo), k4 from CN (2 sts inc'd)

Body Panel

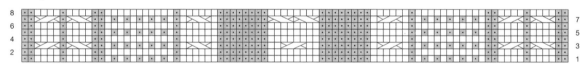

Sleeve Panel

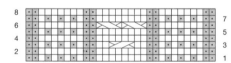

Stag Panel

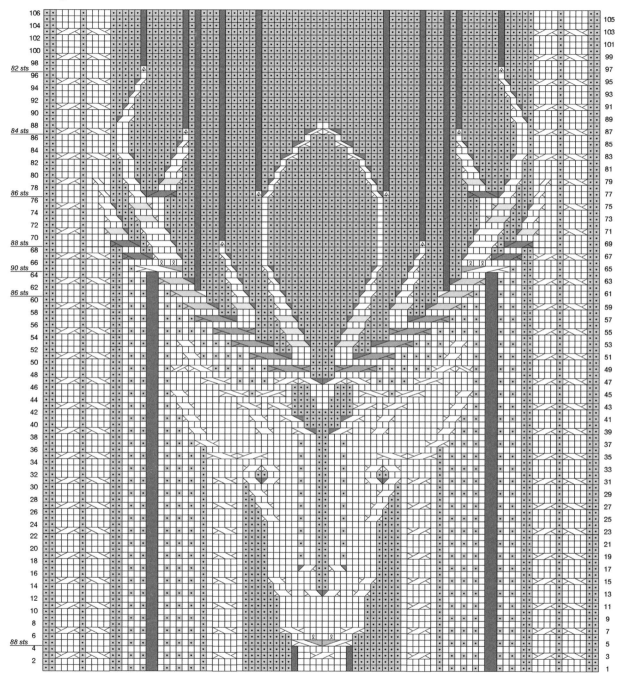

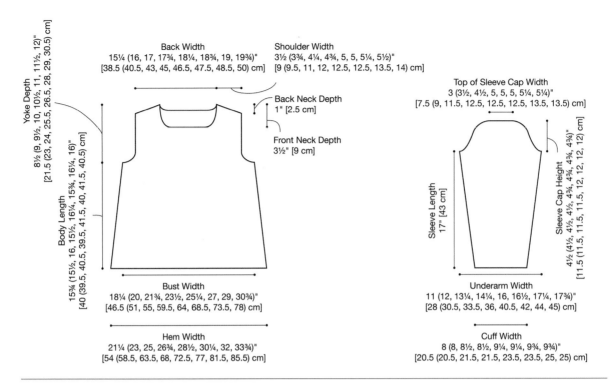

Yoke Depth
8½ (9, 9½, 10, 10½, 11, 11½, 12)"
[21.5 (23, 24, 25.5, 26.5, 28, 29, 30.5) cm]

Back Width
15¼ (16, 17, 17¾, 18¼, 18¾, 19, 19¾)"
[38.5 (40.5, 43, 45, 46.5, 47.5, 48.5, 50) cm]

Shoulder Width
3½ (3¾, 4¼, 4¾, 5, 5, 5¼, 5½)"
[9 (9.5, 11, 12, 12.5, 12.5, 13.5, 14) cm]

Back Neck Depth
1" [2.5 cm]

Front Neck Depth
3½" [9 cm]

Body Length
15¾ (15½, 16, 15½, 16¼, 15¾, 16¼, 16)"
[40 (39.5, 40.5, 39.5, 41.5, 40, 41.5, 40.5) cm]

Bust Width
18¼ (20, 21¾, 23½, 25¼, 27, 29, 30¾)"
[46.5 (51, 55, 59.5, 64, 68.5, 73.5, 78) cm]

Hem Width
21¼ (23, 25, 26¾, 28½, 30¼, 32, 33¾)"
[54 (58.5, 63.5, 68, 72.5, 77, 81.5, 85.5) cm]

Top of Sleeve Cap Width
3 (3½, 4½, 5, 5, 5, 5¼, 5¼)"
[7.5 (9, 11.5, 12.5, 12.5, 12.5, 13.5, 13.5) cm]

Sleeve Length
17" [43 cm]

Sleeve Cap Height
4½ (4½, 4½, 4½, 4¾, 4¾, 4¾, 4¾)"
[11.5 (11.5, 11.5, 11.5, 12, 12, 12, 12) cm]

Underarm Width
11 (12, 13¼, 14¼, 16, 16½, 17¼, 17¾)"
[28 (30.5, 33.5, 36, 40.5, 42, 44, 45) cm]

Cuff Width
8 (8, 8½, 8½, 9¼, 9¼, 9¾, 9¾)"
[20.5 (20.5, 21.5, 21.5, 23.5, 23.5, 25, 25) cm]

Throstle Shawl
Bristol Ivy

I love that birds' wings are an aesthetic paradox: on the one hand (or wing?) they are soft, fluid, organic, malleable. On the other, they are sharp, powerful, and carved in broad architectural strokes. I wanted to capture both sides of that in this shawl by pairing a delicate, feathery, organic lace with crisp garter stitch and graphic short row shaping.

Finished measurements
79" [200.5 cm] wingspan and 19½" [49.5 cm] deep at center

Yarn
Mother by YOTH Yarns
(100% domestic Rambouillet; 100 grams / 550 yards [503 meters])
• 2 skeins in Saba
OR
685 yards [631 meters] in heavy laceweight yarn

Needles
• One 32" [80 cm] circular needle (circ) in size US 4 [3.5 mm]
Or size to obtain gauge

Notions
• Stitch markers
• Tapestry needle

Gauge
21 sts and 40 rows = 4" [10 cm] in garter stitch, after wet-blocking.

Notes
Shawl is worked back and forth from the center back neck out to the hem, with increases occurring within the lace panel and at the outside edges. Short rows are worked twice over the garter stitch wings only. The hem is finished with a picot bind off.

Stitch count in lace will fluctuate within the pattern repeat, as 2 stitches per repeat are added on Row 7 that are then taken away on Row 19. Keep this in mind while counting stitches.

Shawl

Using the long-tail cast on, CO 7 sts. Do not join.
First row: (WS) K3, pm, p1, pm, k3.

Begin garter stitch and chart set up

Next row *inc row:* (RS) K2, yo, knit to m, sl m, work Row 1 of Set-up Chart to m, sl m, knit to last 2 sts, yo, k2 (4 sts inc'd)—11 sts.
Next row: Knit to m, sl m, work next row of chart to m, sl m, knit to end.
Cont in garter st and lace set up as est until Rows 1–12 have been worked one time—35 sts; 9 sts in each side wing, 17 sts in lace.

Begin Lace Chart

Next row *inc row:* (RS) K2, yo, knit to m, sl m, work Row 1 of Lace Chart to m, sl m, knit to last 2 sts, yo, k2 (4 sts inc'd)—39 sts.
Cont as est until Rows 1–20 of Lace Chart have been worked two times—131 sts: 29 sts in each side wing, 73 sts in lace.

Begin short-row shaping

Short Row 1: (RS) K2, yo, knit to 3 sts before m, turn and yo (1 st inc'd)—30 sts in this side wing.
Short Row 2: (WS) Knit to end.
Short Row 3: K2, yo, knit to 3 sts before previous yo, turn and yo (1 st inc'd)—31 sts in this side wing.
Short Row 4: Knit to end.
Rep the last 2 short rows 11 more times—42 sts in this side wing.
Next row: (RS) K2, yo, knit to m, knitting each yo together with its st, sl m, work Row 1 of Lace Chart to m, sl m, knit to last 2 sts, yo, k2 (4 sts inc'd)—148 sts; 43 sts in first side wing, 75 sts in lace, 30 sts in second side wing.

Begin short-row shaping

Short Row 1: (WS) Knit to 3 sts before m, turn and yo;
Short Row 2: (RS) Knit to 2 sts before end, yo, k2 (1 st inc'd)—31 sts in this side wing.

Short Row 3: Knit to 3 sts before previous yo, turn and yo;
Short Row 4: Knit to 2 sts before end, yo, k2 (1 st inc'd)—32 sts in this side wing.
Rep the last 2 short rows 11 more times—43 sts in this side wing.
Next row: (WS) Knit to m, knitting each yo together with its st through the back loop, sl m, work Row 2 of Lace Chart to m, sl m, knit to end.

Continue Body

Next row: (RS) K2, yo, knit to m, sl m, work next row of lace to m, sl m, knit to last 2 sts, yo, k2 (4 sts inc'd)—175 sts.
Cont as est through Row 20 of Lace Chart, then work Rows 1–20 three more times—349 sts; 82 sts in each side wing, 185 sts in lace.

Begin short-row shaping

Short Row 1: (RS) K2, yo, knit to 3 sts before m, turn and yo (1 st inc'd)—83 sts in this side wing.
Short Row 2: (WS) Knit to end.
Short Row 3: K2, yo, knit to 3 sts before previous yo, turn and yo (1 st inc'd)—84 sts in this side wing.
Short Row 4: Knit to end.

Rep the last two short rows 34 more times—118 sts in this side wing.

Next row: (RS) K2, yo, knit to m, knitting each yo together with its st, sl m, work Row 1 of Lace Chart to m, sl m, knit to last 2 sts, yo, k2 (4 sts inc'd)—389 sts: 119 sts in first side wing, 187 sts in lace, 83 sts in second side wing.

Begin short-row shaping
Short Row 1: (WS) Knit to 3 sts before m, knit to 3 sts before m, turn and yo;
Short Row 2: (RS) Knit to 2 sts before end, yo, k2 (1 st inc'd)—84 sts in this side wing.
Short Row 3: Knit to 3 sts before previous yo, turn and yo;
Short Row 4: Knit to 2 sts before end, yo, k2 (1 st inc'd)—85 sts in this side wing.
Rep the last 2 short rows 34 more times—119 sts in this side wing.

Next row: (WS) Knit to m, knitting each yo together with its st through the back loop, sl m, work Row 2 of Lace Chart to m, sl m, knit to end.

End Lace
Next row: (RS) K2, yo, knit to m, sl m, yo, knit to m, yo, sl m, knit to last 2 sts, yo, k2 (4 sts inc'd)—429 sts.
Next row: (WS) Knit.
Rep the last 2 rows two more times—437 sts.
Next row: (RS) Work picot bind off as follows: BO 2 sts, *return st to LH needle, cable CO 2 sts, BO 4 sts; rep from * to end.

Finishing
Weave in ends. Block to measurements.

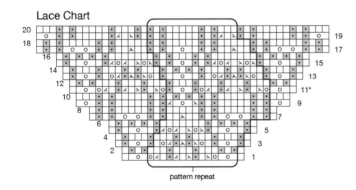

Lace Chart

pattern repeat

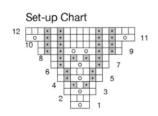

Set-up Chart

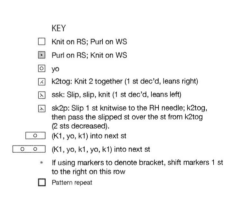

KEY

☐ Knit on RS; Purl on WS

▪ Purl on RS; Knit on WS

○ yo

k2tog: Knit 2 together (1 st dec'd, leans right)

ssk: Slip, slip, knit (1 st dec'd, leans left)

sk2p: Slip 1 st knitwise to the RH needle; k2tog, then pass the slipped st over the st from k2tog (2 sts decreased).

(K1, yo, k1) into next st

(K1, yo, k1, yo, k1) into next st

* If using markers to denote bracket, shift markers 1 st to the right on this row

☐ Pattern repeat

Nepali Bird Vest
by Carol Sunday

A friend and photographer who traveled to Nepal and the upper Himalayas brought back a photo of a sadhu novice (sage-in-training) with a bird perched on her head. It was a delightful picture and has stuck in my head. I'm also quite taken with the traditional garments from the region, which seem designed for comfort whether trekking or meditating or anything in between. Cord ties are often used in place of buttons or zippers—a softer, gentler kind of closure.

Finished measurements
30 (34, 38¼, 42½, 46¾, 51, 55¼)" [76 (86.5, 97.5, 108, 118.5, 129.5, 140) cm] bust circumference; shown in size 34" [86.5 cm] with 0 ease.
Suggested ease: -3 to +1" [-7.5 to 2.5 cm] ease

Yarn
Nirvana 5 ply by Sunday Knits
(90% merino wool / 10% cashmere: 50 grams / 137 yards [125 meters])
• 5 (6, 7, 8, 8, 9, 10) skeins in Earth
OR
670 (780, 880, 990, 1100, 1210, 1310) yards [620 (710, 810, 910, 1010, 1110, 1200) meters] in worsted weight or other Sunday Knits 5 ply yarn

Needles
• One pair of straight needles, or one 32" [80 cm] circular needle (circ) in size US 7 [4.5 mm]
• One 32" [80 cm] circular needle (circ) in size US 6 [4 mm]
• One set double-pointed needle (dpns) in sizes US 5 and US 7 [3.75 and 4.5 mm]
• One crochet hook in size US 4/E [3.5 mm]
Or sizes to obtain gauge

Notions
• Stitch markers
• Locking stitch markers
• Stitch holders or waste yarn
• Tapestry needle
• CC yarn for Sunday Short Rows

Gauge
19 sts and 26 rows = 4" [10 cm] in stockinette stitch with larger needles, after blocking.

Notes
Vest is worked flat in one piece to the underarms, then front and back are worked separately to shoulder and joined using the three-needle bind off. Stitches are picked up along upper front and back neck and worked in a Nehru-style lapel. I-cord ties are knit and then joined with the upper body, and underarms are trimmed with an applied I-cord. Crochet chain loops are added at sides for securing ties. Straight needles may be used, as the piece is worked flat, but larger sizes may prefer circular needles to accommodate the number of stitches.

I-cord ties (make 2)
With smaller dpns and using the long-tail cast on, CO 3 sts.
Work in I-cord for 14-15" [35-38 cm]. Cut yarn. Leave on dpn and set aside to be attached later.

Vest
With larger needles and using the long-tail cast on, CO 171 (191, 211, 231, 251, 271, 291) sts.
Do not join.

Begin at bottom
First row: (WS) P3, knit to last 3 sts, p3.
Next row: (RS) K3, p1, knit to last 4 sts, p1, k3.
Rep the last two rows one more time.
Next row: (WS) P3, k1, purl to last 4 sts, k1, p3.

Begin Border pattern
Note: Place markers for each repeat of Border pattern, if you like.
Next row: (RS) K3, p1, k1, work Row 1 of Border pattern to last 5 sts, k1, p1, k3.
Next row: (WS) P3, k1, p1, work next row of Border pattern to last 5 sts, p1, k1, p3.
Cont as est until Rows 1–30 of Border pattern have been worked one time.

Begin Bird pattern
Next row: Work 5 sts as est, work Row 1 of Bird pattern to last 5 sts, work 5 sts as est.

Cont edge sts and Bird pattern as est until pc meas 10¾ (11, 11¼, 11½, 11½, 11½, 11½)" [27.5 (28, 28.5, 29, 29, 29, 29) cm], ending after a RS row.
Next row: (WS) Work 50 (55, 60, 65, 70, 75, 80) sts as est, pm for side, work 71 (81, 91, 101, 111, 121, 131) sts, pm for side, place 3rd marker to leave in place for measuring later, work as est to end.

Begin side shaping
Note: Increases are worked on the fronts only, and always in stockinette sections so that any birds worked near the side edges will maintain their shape.
Next row *inc row:* (RS) Work as est to last knit st before side m, k1/L, if necessary, cont in patt to side m, sl m, work as est to next side m, sl m, if necessary, work in patt to next knit st, k1/R, work as est to end (2 sts inc'd)—173 (193, 213, 233, 253, 273, 293) sts.
Rep *inc row* every 4 rows four more times—181 (201, 221, 241, 261, 281, 301) sts.
Work WS row.

Attach I-cord ties
With RS facing and working yarn in back, place sts for I-cord onto LN (left needle). Bring working yarn behind I-cord sts, ready to work next row.
Next row: (RS) K2, ssk, return these 3 sts to LN.
Next row: (RS) K2, ssk, return these 3 sts to LN.
Next row: (RS) K2, ssk, p1, k1, work in Bird pattern to last 5 sts, work edge sts as est.
With WS facing and working yarn in front, place sts for I-cord onto LH needle. Bring working yarn in front of I-cord sts, ready to work next row.
Next row: (WS) P2, p2tog, return these 3 sts to LN.
Next row: (WS) P2, p2tog, return these 3 sts to LN.
Next row: (WS) P2, p2tog, k1, p1, work bird patt to last 5 sts, work edge sts as est.

Continue side shaping and begin center front shaping
Next row *front dec and side inc row:* (RS) K3, p1, k2tog, work as est to last knit st before side m, k1/L, if necessary, cont in patt to side m, sl m, work as est to next side m, sl m, if necessary, work in patt to next knit st, k1/R, work as est to last 6 sts, ssk, p1, k3 (2 front edge sts dec'd, 2 side sts inc'd).
Next row: (WS) P3, k1, p1, work to last 5 sts, p1, k1, p3.

Next row *front dec row:* (RS) K3, p1, k2tog, work as est to last 6 sts, ssk, p1, k3 (2 front edge sts dec'd)—179 (199, 219, 239, 259, 279, 299) sts rem.
Work 1 WS row.
Rep the last 4 rows three more times—175 (195, 215, 235, 255, 275, 295) sts.
Work WS row.

Divide for Fronts and Back
Note: To avoid the gap between the first bound-off stitch and the stitch before it, work as est to 1 st before bind off, k1-f/b, k1, pass the second st on RH needle over the first. This does NOT count as a bound off stitch, but does count as the first of the 2 knit sts that are worked when beginning to bind off.

Next row *underarm BO:* (RS) K3, p1, k2tog, work as est to 4 (6, 7, 8, 9, 10, 12) sts before side m, BO 8 (12, 14, 16, 18, 20, 24) sts, work to 4 (6, 7, 8, 9, 10, 12) sts before next m, BO 8 (12, 14, 16, 18, 20, 24) sts, work as est to last 6 sts, ssk, p1, k3 (2 sts dec'd)—63 (69, 77, 85, 93, 101, 107) sts rem for back and 47 (50, 54, 58, 62, 66, 69) sts for each front. Place sts for Back and Right Front onto waste yarn or st holder. Make note of last row worked in Bird pattern.

Left Front
Next row: (WS) Work as est to last st, k1-tbl. Break yarn.

Begin underarm I-cord
A section of applied I-cord is worked from center of underarm to Left Front armhole edge, to be continued with left front as edge trim. Use any cast on method you prefer.

With new yarn and larger dpns, CO 3 sts, then, with RS facing, pick up 1 st at center of left underarm. With yarn in back, slide sts to other end of dpn, ready to work next RS row.
Next row: (RS) K2, ssk, pick up next underarm st, then slide sts to other end of dpn, ready to work next RS row.
Rep the last row for each underarm st, then slip 4 sts onto working needle with Left Front sts—51 (54, 58, 62, 66, 70, 73).

Final applied I-cord row: (RS) K2, ssk, p1, k2tog, work as est to to last 6 sts, ssk, p1, k3 (3 sts dec'd)—48 (51, 55, 59, 63, 67, 70) sts rem.
Next row: (WS) Work as est to last 5 sts, p1, k1, p3.

Begin armhole shaping

Note: Continue in Bird pattern when possible while decreasing. Use your own discretion when beginning a partial bird on a decrease edge.

Center front decreases are continued every RS row throughout front to shoulder shaping, and setup for lapel will take place before armhole shaping is completed. Please read ahead carefully before beginning.

Next row *armhole dec row:* (RS) K3, p1, k2tog, work Bird pattern and front dec as est (1 st dec'd at armhole edge).

Rep front dec every RS row as est, and AT THE SAME TIME, rep a*rmhole dec row* every RS row 0 (1, 3, 5, 7, 10, 12) more time(s), then every 4 rows three times, and AT THE SAME TIME, when pc meas 2¾ (3, 3¼, 3½, 3½, 3¾, 3¾)" [7 (7.5, 8, 8.5, 9, 9.5, 10) cm] from underarm, on the next RS row, setup for lapel as follows:

Set up for Lapel

Next row: (RS) Work as est, with armhole dec if required, to last 6 sts, ssk, p1, place 3 rem sts onto waste yarn or st holder for Lapel. Make note of last row worked in Bird pattern.
Next row: (WS) P2, work as est to end.

Establish new front neck decrease

Next row *new center front dec row:* (RS) Work as est, with armhole dec if required, to last 3 sts, ssk, k1 (1 st dec'd at neck edge).
Next row: (WS) P2, work as est to end.

Cont as est, working any rem armhole dec rows for your size, and working *new center front dec row* every RS row, until 18 (18, 19, 19, 19, 19, 19) sts rem, ending after a RS row.

Armhole meas approx 7¾ (8¼, 8¾, 9¼, 9¾, 10¼, 10½)" [19.5 (21, 22, 23.5, 25, 26, 26.5) cm] from underarm. Make note of last row worked in Bird pattern.

Begin shoulder shaping

Cont *new center front dec row* every RS row as est while working short rows until 14 (14, 15, 15, 15, 15, 15, 15) sts rem.

Short Row 1: (WS) Work as est to last 3 sts, turn work, place one strip of CC yarn across working yarn as for a Sunday Short Row (See Techniques, pg 152).
Short Row 2: (RS) Work as est to end.
Short Row 3: Work to 2 sts before previous turning point (where CC yarn was placed), turn work, place one strip of CC yarn across working yarn.
Short Row 4: Work as est to end.

Rep Short Rows 3 and 4 four more times.
Next row: (WS) Work to end of row and resolve short rows as for a WS row.
Place sts onto waste yarn or st holder.

Back

Transfer sts for back to larger needles, ready to work a RS row.

Begin underarm I-cord

With larger dpn and RS facing, beg at center of left underarm (beside I-cord CO from left front), pick up 1 st in underarm, then pick up 3 sts from I-cord CO. With yarn in back, slide sts to other end of dpn, ready to work next RS row.

First row: (RS) K2tog, k2, slide sts to other end of dpn, ready to work next RS row, then pick up next underarm st.
Rep the last row for each underarm st.
Next row: (RS) K2tog, k2, turn work and slip 3 sts onto working needle with back sts, ready to work a WS row.
Next row: (WS) P3, k1-tbl, work next row of bird pattern to last 2 sts, p1, k1-tbl.

With new yarn and larger dpns, CO 3 sts, then, with RS facing, pick up 1 st at center of right underarm. With yarn in back, slide sts to other end of dpn, ready to work next RS row.

Next row: (RS) K2, ssk, pick up next underarm st, then slide sts to other end of dpn, ready to work next RS row.

Rep the last row for each underarm st, then slip 4 sts onto working needle with Back sts—70 (76, 84, 92, 100, 108, 114) sts. Break yarn. Cont with yarn attached at back.

Final applied I-cord row: (RS) K2, ssk, p1, k2tog, work as est to to last 6 sts, ssk, p1, k3 (3 sts dec'd)—67 (73, 81, 89, 97, 105, 111) sts rem.

Next row: (WS) P3, k1, p1, work to last 5 sts, p1, k1, p3.

Begin armhole shaping

Next row *dec row:* (RS) K3, p1, k2tog, p1, k2tog, work as est to last 6 sts, ssk, p1, k3 (2 sts dec'd)—65 (71, 79, 87, 95, 103, 109) sts rem.

Rep *dec row* every RS row 0 (1, 3, 5, 7, 10, 12) more times, then every 4th row three times—59 (63, 67, 71, 75, 77, 79) sts rem.

Work even until back meas approx 7¾ (8¼, 8¾, 9¼, 9¾, 10¼, 10½)" [19.5 (21, 22, 23.5, 25, 26, 26.5) cm] from underarm, ending on row noted in Left Front.

Begin shoulder shaping

Short Row 1: (WS) Work as est to last 5 sts, turn work, place one strip of CC yarn across working yarn as for a Sunday Short Row.

Short Row 2: (RS) Work as est to last 5 sts, turn work, place one strip of CC yarn across working yarn as for a Sunday Short Row.

Short Row 3: Work to 3 sts before previous turning point (where CC yarn was placed), turn work, place one strip of CC yarn across working yarn.

Short Row 4: Work to 3 sts before previous turning point (where CC yarn was placed), turn work, place one strip of CC yarn across working yarn.

Rep Short Rows 3 and 4 one more time.

Next row: (WS) Work to end of row and resolve short rows as for a WS row.

Next row: Work to end of row and resolve short rows as for a RS row.

Place sts onto waste yarn or st holder.

Right Front

Transfer sts for Right Front to larger needles, ready to work a RS row.

Begin underarm I-cord

With larger dpn and RS facing, beg at center of right underarm (beside I-cord CO from left front), pick up 1 st in underarm, then pick up 3 sts from I-cord CO. With yarn in back, slide sts to other end of dpn, ready to work next RS row.

First row: (RS) K2tog, k2, slide sts to other end of dpn, ready to work next RS row, then pick up next underarm st.

Rep the last row for each underarm st.

Final applied I-cord row: K2, k2tog, turn work and slip 3 sts onto working needle with back sts, ready to work a WS row.

Next row: (WS) P3, k1-tbl, work next row of bird pattern to last 5 sts, p1, k1, p3.

Begin armhole shaping

Center front decreases are continued throughout front to shoulder shaping, and setup for Lapel will take place before armhole shaping is completed. Please read ahead carefully before beginning.

Next row *armhole dec row:* (RS) Work front dec and Bird pattern as est to last 6 sts, ssk, p1, k3. (1 st dec'd at armhole edge).

Rep front dec every RS row, and AT THE SAME TIME, rep *armhole dec row* every RS row 1 (2, 4, 6, 8, 11, 13) more time(s), then every 4 rows three times, and AT THE SAME TIME, when pc meas 2¾ (3, 3¼, 3½, 3½, 3¾, 3¾)" [7 (7.5, 8, 8.5, 9, 9.5, 10 cm] from underarm, having just worked row noted from Left Front Lapel placement, setup for lapel as follows:

Set up for Lapel

Next row: (WS) Work as est to last 4 sts, p1, place 3 rem sts onto waste yarn or st holder for Lapel.

Establish new front neck decrease

Next row *new center front dec row:* (RS) K1, k2tog, work as est, with armhole dec if required, to end (1 st dec'd at neck edge).

Next row: (WS) Work as est to last 2 sts, p2.

Cont as est, working any rem armhole dec rows for your size, and working *new center front dec row* every RS row, until 18 (18, 19, 19, 19, 19, 19) sts rem, ending one row after row noted in Left Front. Armhole meas approx 7¾ (8¼, 8¾, 9¼, 9¾, 10¼, 10½)" [19.5 (21, 22, 23.5, 25, 26, 26.5) cm] from underarm.

Begin shoulder shaping

Cont *new center front dec row* every every RS row while working short rows until 14 (14, 15, 15, 15, 15, 15, 15) sts rem.

Short Row 1: (RS) Work as est to last 3 sts, turn work, place one strip of CC yarn across working yarn as for a Sunday Short Row.

Short Row 2: (WS) Work as est to end.

Short Row 3: Work to 2 sts before previous turning point (where CC yarn was placed), turn work, place one strip of CC yarn across working yarn.

Short Row 4: Work as est to end.

Rep Short Rows 3 and 4 four more times.

Next row: (WS) Work to end of row and resolve short rows as for a RS row.

Join Shoulders

Transfer sts held for back to smaller circ. With RS together, beg at right armhole edge, and using the three-needle bind off, BO all right front sts with corresponding back sts, then BO 31 (35, 37, 41, 45, 47, 49) back sts, then transfer left front sts to larger needle so that needle tip is at neck edge and with RS together, using the three-needle bind off, BO all rem sts.

Finishing

Weave in ends. Block to measurements.

Lapel

With RS facing and smaller circ, place 3 held sts from right front to RH needle, pick up and knit 1 st in each row along right front, pick up and knit 1 st in each BO st at back neck, then pick up and knit 1 st in each row to held sts at left front, then place the 3 held sts onto RH needle.

Next row: (WS) Sl 2 wyif, p1, k1-tbl, purl to lasts 4 sts, k1 tbl, p1, sl 2 wyif.

Next row: (RS) Sl 1 wyib, k2, p1, work Row 1 of Border pattern to last 4 sts, making note of last st in patt worked, p1, k2, sl wyib.

Next row: P3, k1, beg with pattern st noted from previous row, work next row of Border pattern to last 4 sts (ending with first st of patt), k1, p3.

Next row: K3, p1, cont patt as est to last 4 sts, p1, k3.

Cont edge sts and Border pattern as est until Rows 1–8 of Border have been worked one time.

Next row: (RS) K3, p1, knit to last 4 sts, p1, k3.

Next row: P3, k1, purl to last 4 sts, k1, p3.

I-cord bind off

Use larger needle or dpn to work bind off.

Next row: (RS) K1, sl 1 wyib, turn work.

Next row: (WS) P2.

Right Side

Work I-cord bind off as follows: (RS) *K2, ssk, return 3 sts to LH needle; rep from * to center of back neck.

Slide all sts to other end of circ. Join yarn, ready to work a WS row.

Left Side

Use larger needle or dpn to work bind off.

Next row: (WS) P1, sl 1 wyif, turn work.

Next row: (RS) K2.

Work I-cord bind off as follows: (WS) P2, p2tog, return 3 sts to LH needle; rep from * until 7 sts rem; 3 sts each from left and right cord and 1 unworked st.

With WS together, beg at neck edge, use the Kitchener stitch to join left and right sides, working the final odd st together with the st beside it.

Closure loops

Locate position at side of Left Front where tie should be secured. (If unsure, just above the beg of side shaping is a good spot.) With a locking st marker, mark on the RS of fabric. Rep for Right Front, placing marker on WS of fabric.

With crochet hook, make a sl st into the fabric at marker, ch for 1" [2.5 cm], then sl st into fabric approx ¾" [2 cm] away from starting point, turn and sl st in each ch st to beg. Draw yarn through final st and secure to WS of fabric.

Rep for second loop.

Weave in ends. Block again, if you desired.

Carol is a country mouse, a knitwear designer, the owner of Sunday Knits Yarns, and the creator of the popular Sunday Short Rows technique.
www.sundayknits.com Instagram: carolsundayknits

Nepali Bird Vest

Bird pattern

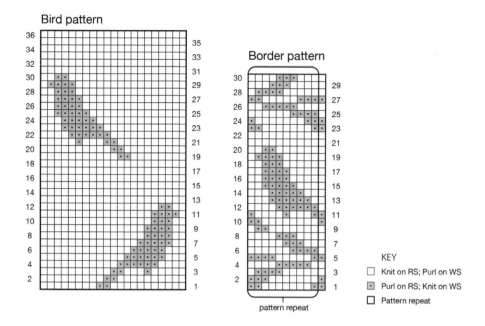

Border pattern

KEY

☐ Knit on RS; Purl on WS

⊡ Purl on RS; Knit on WS

☐ Pattern repeat

pattern repeat

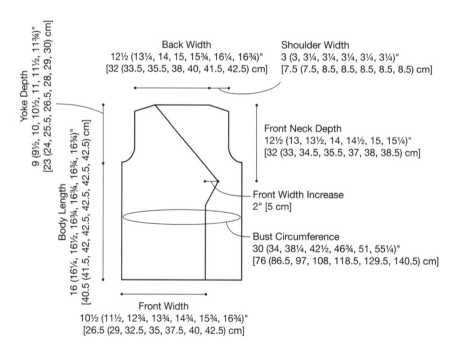

Yoke Depth
9 (9½, 10, 10½, 11, 11½, 11¾)"
[23 (24, 25.5, 26.5, 28, 29, 30) cm]

Body Length
16 (16¼, 16½, 16¾, 16¾, 16¾, 16¾)"
[40.5 (41.5, 42, 42.5, 42.5, 42.5, 42.5) cm]

Back Width
12½ (13¼, 14, 15, 15¾, 16¼, 16¾)"
[32 (33.5, 35.5, 38, 40, 41.5, 42.5) cm]

Shoulder Width
3 (3, 3¼, 3¼, 3¼, 3¼, 3¼)"
[7.5 (7.5, 8.5, 8.5, 8.5, 8.5, 8.5) cm]

Front Neck Depth
12½ (13, 13½, 14, 14½, 15, 15¼)"
[32 (33, 34.5, 35.5, 37, 38, 38.5) cm]

Front Width Increase
2" [5 cm]

Bust Circumference
30 (34, 38¼, 42½, 46¾, 51, 55¼)"
[76 (86.5, 97, 108, 118.5, 129.5, 140.5) cm]

Front Width
10½ (11½, 12¾, 13¾, 14¾, 15¾, 16¾)"
[26.5 (29, 32.5, 35, 37.5, 40, 42.5) cm]

Nyla Hat
by Cal Patch

Animals have always felt kindred to me. As a child, I had nearly every kind of pet I could get my hands on, including rodents of all sorts, an aquarium with tropical fish, shrimp, eels and frogs, the essential cats and dogs of course, hermit crabs, a rabbit, and even a horse. I've also been a vegetarian—of varying degrees—since I was a teenager. So, as a clothing designer and fiber/textile lover, I've always had a great deal of conflict over the idea of fur. In principle I'm against it, but I can't deny that I have always been drawn to it as well. Fur is one factor that makes us love animals: soft, exotic, tactile…and wearing it seems such a good way to get just a little closer to being one.

For the most part, avoiding fur hasn't been difficult. A posh fur coat doesn't attract me at all. But often, at fiber festivals, there will be a booth selling enormously fluffy alpaca, or shearling, or rabbit skin hats. You know, the kind with earflaps, that look like they'd keep you cozy at Arctic temperatures. These hats have always been a weakness, and I've spent much time trying them on, coveting, and hemming and hawing over them, though I've never actually come fully around to the idea of buying one, because they are still…fur.

The crochet loop stitch, when cut, can become a shaggy, plush, fur-like texture. Not every yarn will achieve the effect; it must be a plump, low-twist, wooly single-ply, or you might end up with something resembling chopped-up spaghetti rather than a sheep's fleece. Puffin worked exactly as I hoped, and fulfilled the vision in my head of a warm hat that looks like shearling but is, in fact, crocheted from yarn, and thus made with no harm to the sheep. It can be worn with the fleece side in or out. I named the hat Nyla because she is the female character in the fascinating 1920's documentary, *Nanook of the North*, and knows how to keep warm!

Finished measurements
24¾" [63 cm] brim circumference and 10¼" [26 cm] height from brim to crown
To fit a 22-23" head. Notes on adjusting size are included in pattern.

Yarn
Puffin by Quince & Co.
(100% American wool; 100 grams / 112 yards [102 meters])
• 2 skeins Caspian
OR
112 yards [102 meters] in chunky weight yarn

Hook
• One hook in size J/10 [6 mm]
Or size to obtain gauge

Notions
• Scrap yarn or split ring stitch marker
• Tapestry needle

Gauge
11 sts and 9 rnds = 4" [10 cm] in Loop Half-Double-Crochet, after blocking.

Special Stitches
lhdc (loop half double crochet): This is essentially the common "loop st" but with an extra yarn over, making it more of a hdc than a sc for a taller st. To make it: yo and insert hook into indicated st, place a finger behind st so yarn is wrapped around it, forming the "loop" on back of work (keep finger there until st is completed), yo and pull through st (you will now have 3 loops on the hook), yo and pull through 3 loops. St is now complete and you can take your finger out of the loop on the back side of work.

flhdc (front loop half double crochet): This is the same as the loop half double crochet, but loop is made on the front of work instead of the back. To make it: push your thumb against the working yarn and toward you, forming a loop (keep thumb in place until st is completed), yo and insert hook into st, yo and pull through st (you will now have 3 loops on the hook), yo and pull through 3 loops. St is now complete and you can take your thumb out of the loop on the front side of work.

lhdc2tog (loop half double crochet 2 together): Yo and insert hook into st, place a finger behind st so yarn is wrapped around it, forming the "loop" on back of work, yo and pull through st (you will now have 3 loops on the hook), yo and insert hook into next st, place a finger behind st so yarn is wrapped around it, forming a second "loop" on back of work, yo and pull through st (you will now have 4 loops on the hook), yo and pull through 4 loops. This creates a decrease, worked in the lhdc st.

flhdc2tog (front loop half double crochet 2 together): Push your thumb against the working yarn and toward you, forming a loop in front of work, yo and insert hook into st, yo and pull through st (you will now have 3 loops on the hook), push your thumb against the working yarn and toward you, forming a second loop in front of work, yo and insert hook into next st, yo and pull through st (you will now have 4 loops on the hook), yo and pull through 4 loops. This creates a decrease, worked in the flhdc st.

Notes

Hat is worked from top down in spiraling rnds, without joining. For this reason, it's important to use a marker to help you identify the end of each rnd and beginning of next rnd. I usually use a piece of scrap yarn that I carry through the last st of every rnd, but a split ring or any st marker that opens will work.

To adjust size up or down: The first 11 rounds of the pattern are increase rounds, with two of those rounds (8 and 10) toward the end having no increases, to slow the rate of increase before it stops completely. You can easily make a smaller or larger hat by working fewer, or more, increase rounds. At least one round of "work even" on a baby/child's hat, or two rounds on an adult hat (with an increase round in between), before the final increase round, will help blend the shaping into the rest of the hat.

Hat

Crown Shaping

Rnd 1: Ch 3 (does not count as a st), work 8 lhdc into 3rd ch from hook—8 sts.
Cont working in the rnd, without joining at the end of each rnd. Place marker in last st to mark end of rnd. Move marker up on the last st of every following rnd.
Rnd 2: *2 lhdc into next st; rep from * around—16 sts.
Rnd 3: *2 lhdc in next st, lhdc in next st; rep from * around—24 sts.

Rnd 4: *2 lhdc in first st, lhdc in each of next 2 sts; repeat from * around—32 sts.
Rnd 5: *2 lhdc in first st, lhdc in each of next 3 sts; rep from * around—40 sts.
Rnd 6: *2 lhdc in first st, lhdc in each of next 4 sts; rep from * around—48 sts.
Rnd 7: *2 lhdc in first st, lhdc in each of next 5 sts; rep from * around—56 sts.
Rnd 8: Lhdc in each st around.
Rnd 9: *2 lhdc in first st, lhdc in each of next 6 sts; rep from * around—64 sts.
Rnd 10: Lhdc in each st around.
Rnd 11: *2 lhdc in first st, lhdc in each of next 15 sts; rep from * around—68 sts.
Rnds 12–18: Lhdc in each st around.

First Earflap

Row 1: 14 lhdc, turn—14 sts.
Row 2: Ch 2 (does not count as a st), sk first st, flhdc2tog, 9 flhdc, flhdc2tog—11 sts rem.
Row 3: Ch 2, sk first st, lhdc2tog, 6 lhdc, lhdc2tog—8 sts rem.
Row 4: Ch 2, sk first st, flhdc2tog, 3 flhdc, flhdc2tog—5 sts rem.
Row 5: Ch 2, sk first st, lhdc2tog twice—2 sts rem. Fasten off.

Second Earflap

Looking at the hat with loops on the inside, from left side edge of first earflap, sk 26 sts and join into next st with a sl st.
Row 1: Ch 2, lhdc in first st and next 13 sts, turn—14 sts.
Rows 2–5: Same as first earflap. Fasten off.

Edging

Join with a sl st into any st between the two earflaps in back (the back is the smaller space between earflaps). Ch 1, sc into first st and every st around, join with sl st and finish off.

Finishing

Weave in all ends.

Cut Loops

Starting from the top, and working around in rows, insert scissors into 3 or more loops at a time and give them a tug to tighten, then cut loops open. Continue until all loops are cut.

Nyla Hat Blocking

Note: This is how I blocked my hat in the Puffin yarn, which is very fluffy and wooly, and held together well. If your yarn is more slippery, you may wish to block the hat once BEFORE cutting the loops, to set them in place, then block it again. Test on a swatch first. Slippery yarn could unravel if the loops are cut before blocking.

Soak hat in tepid water for 30 minutes. Roll in a towel to remove as much water as possible, and allow to air-dry flat, being careful not to stretch it out. Periodically turn it inside out and turn it to help it dry more quickly.

Cal is a crochet designer and author of Design-It-Yourself Clothes: Patternmaking Simplified. *She lives on a farm in NY.*
www.hodgepodgefarm.net Instagram: hodgepodgefarm

Town-O Cap
Beatrice Perron Dahlen

Town-O Cap is inspired by a fox's tail, tipped in white. Its name comes from one of my favorite children's songs, *The Fox*, an old folk song;

"The fox went out on a chilly night,
he prayed to the Moon to give him light,
for he'd many a mile to go that night
before he reached the town-o, town-o, town-o,
he had many a mile to go that night
before he reached the town-o."

Finished measurements
15 (17, 18¾, 19¾, 20¾, 21¾)" [38 (43, 47.5, 50, 52.5, 55) cm] brim circumference
6¾ (7, 7¼, 8¼, 8¼, 8¾)" [17 (18, 18.5, 21, 21, 22) cm] height from brim to crown
To fit sizes: Child's 3–12 mos (12 mos–4 years, 4 years–12 years, Adult S, M, L)

Yarn
Lark by Quince and Co.
(100% American wool; 50 grams / 134 yards [123 meters])

For cap with CC crown:
• 1 skein in Fox (MC)
• 1 skein in Audouin (CC)
OR MC: 69 (83, 92, 114, 120, 132) yards [63 (76, 84, 104, 110, 121) meters]; CC: 35 (40, 50, 58, 61, 70) yards [32 (37, 46, 53, 56, 64 meters]
For solid cap:
• 1 (1, 2, 2, 2, 2) skeins OR 104 (122, 141, 172, 180, 202) yards [95 (112, 129, 157, 165, 185) meters] excluding the pom pom
• Scrap ball of yarn for pom pom

Needles
• One 16" [40 cm] circular needle (circ) in size US 5 [3.75 mm]
• One set double pointed needles (dpns) in size US 5 [3.75 mm]
Or size to obtain gauge

Notions
• Tapestry needle
• Stitch marker
• Pom pom maker (optional), or tools for making pom pom

Gauge
17 sts and 26 brioche rnds = 4" [10 cm] in Brioche Stitch, after blocking. (See Notes on row gauge.)

K1, yf sl1yo: Knit 1, bring yarn under the right needle to the front, slip the next st purlwise, then bring the yarn over the right needle and across the slipped st to the back of the needle.

Sl1yof, brp: With yarn in front, slip the next st purlwise, then bring the yarn over and across the st, and then back to the front. Purl the next st and its yo (a brp).

Brk, yf sl1yo: Knit the next st with its yo (a brk). Bring yarn under the right hand needle to the front, slip the next st purlwise, then bring the yarn over the needle and across the slipped st to the back of the needle.

Notes
When measuring the row gauge in Brioche Stitch, 2 rnds look like 1 rnd and are therefore referred to as a brioche rnd. Row gauge is not critical for this pattern.

Cap
With circ, MC, and using the long-tail cast on, CO 64 (72, 80, 84, 88, 92) sts. Place marker (pm) and join to work in the rnd, being careful not to twist sts.

Begin Brioche Stitch (multiple of 2 sts)
Set-up rnd: *K1, yf sl1yo; rep from * to end.
Rnd 1: *Sl1yof, brp; rep from * to end.
Rnd 2: *Brk, yf sl1yo; rep from * to end.
Rep Rnds 1 and 2 until piece meas 3¾ (4, 4, 4¾, 4¾, 5)" [9.5 (10, 10, 12, 12, 12.5) cm] from beg, ending after Rnd 1 of Brioche Stitch.

If making the version with a CC at the crown, change yarn to CC. Cont in patt until piece meas 4½ (4¾, 5, 6, 6, 6½)" [11.5 (12, 12.5, 15, 15, 16.5) cm] from beg, ending after rnd 2 of patt.
Next rnd: *Brk1, p1; rep from * to end.
Next rnd: *K1, p1; rep from * to end.
Rep the last Rnd one more time.

Begin Crown Shaping
Change to dpns when sts no longer fit comfortably on circ.
Knit 2 rnds.
Next rnd *dec rnd 1:* *K2, k2tog; rep from * to end (16 (18, 20, 21, 22, 23) sts dec'd)—48 (54, 60, 63, 66, 69) sts rem.
Knit 3 rnds.
Next rnd *dec rnd 2:* *K1, k2tog; rep from * to end (16 (18, 20, 21, 22, 23) sts dec'd)—32 (36, 40, 42, 44, 46) sts rem.
Knit 3 rnds.
Next rnd *dec rnd 3:* *K2tog; rep from * to end (16 (18, 20, 21, 22, 23) sts dec'd)—16 (18, 20, 21, 22, 23) sts rem.

Knit 1 rnd.
Next rnd *dec rnd 4:* [K2tog] 8 (9, 10, 10, 11, 11) times, knit to end if necessary (8 (9, 10, 10, 11, 11) sts dec'd)—8 (9, 10, 11, 11, 12) sts rem.
Leaving a long tail, cut yarn and pull through rem sts.

Finishing
Weave in ends. Block if desired.
Make a pom pom if desired.

Simple Pillow
Carrie Bostick Hoge

This pillow was used for Tif Fussell's Woolly Tattooing project, pages 12–15.

Finished measurements
17¼" [44 cm] wide and 17¾" [45 cm] high
Yarn
Lark by Quince & Co.
(100% American wool; 50 grams / 134 yards [123 meters])
• 6 skeins in Bark
OR
735 yards [677 meters] in worsted weight yarn
Needles
• One 29" [74 mm] circular needle (circ) each in sizes US 5 and 6 [3.75 and 4 mm]
• One spare circ in size US 6 [4 mm]
Or sizes to obtain gauge
Notions
• Tapestry needle
• 6 buttons, ¾" [19 mm]
• Pillow form, 18" [45.5 cm] square

Gauge
20 sts and 28 rnds = 4" [10 cm] with larger needles, after blocking.

Pillow
With larger circ and a provisional cast on or waste yarn, CO 172 sts. Pm and join to work in the rnd, careful not to twist sts.

Begin stockinette stitch
First rnd: Knit.
Cont in St st until pillow meas 17¾" [45 cm] from beg.

Next rnd: K86, bind off rem sts.
Change to smaller circ.

Begin garter stitch flap
Note: Work flap back and forth in rows.
Next row: (WS) Knit.
Cont in garter st until flap meas 2¾" [7 cm] from first garter ridge, ending after a WS row.

Begin buttonhole rows
Next row: (RS) K7, *k2tog, [yo] two times, k2tog, k8; rep from * five more times, k7 to end.
Next row: (WS) *Knit to first buttonhole, knit into first wrap, knit through the back loop of second wrap; rep from * five more times, knit to end.
Cont in garter st for 1" [2.5 cm], ending after a RS row.
Next row: (WS) BO all sts knitwise.

Finishing
Weave in ends. Block to measurements.

Unzip waste yarn and place first 86 sts onto larger circ, then place rem 86 sts onto spare needle.
With RS together and using the three-needle bind off, BO all sts.

Sew buttons onto back of pillow, opposite buttonholes.

Bird template for pie
by Tammy White
pages 44–47

Bee template for Covered Journal with Cross-Stitch
by Lori Ann Graham
pages 9–11

Bee template for Tote
by Beatrice Perron Dahlen
pages 16–17

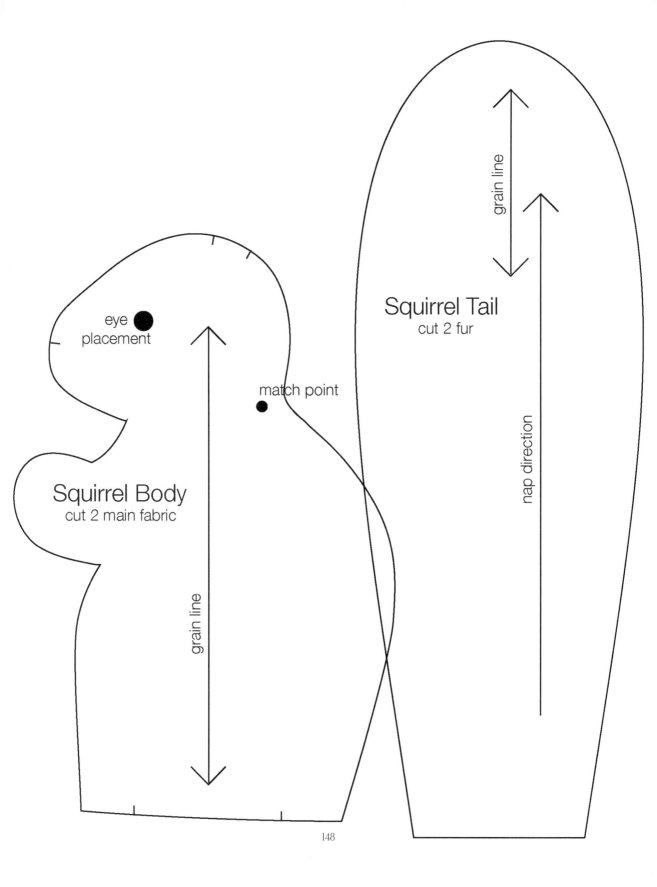

eye
placement

match point

Squirrel Body
cut 2 main fabric

grain line

Squirrel Tail
cut 2 fur

grain line

nap direction

Squirrel template / project by Grainline Studio
pages 68–70

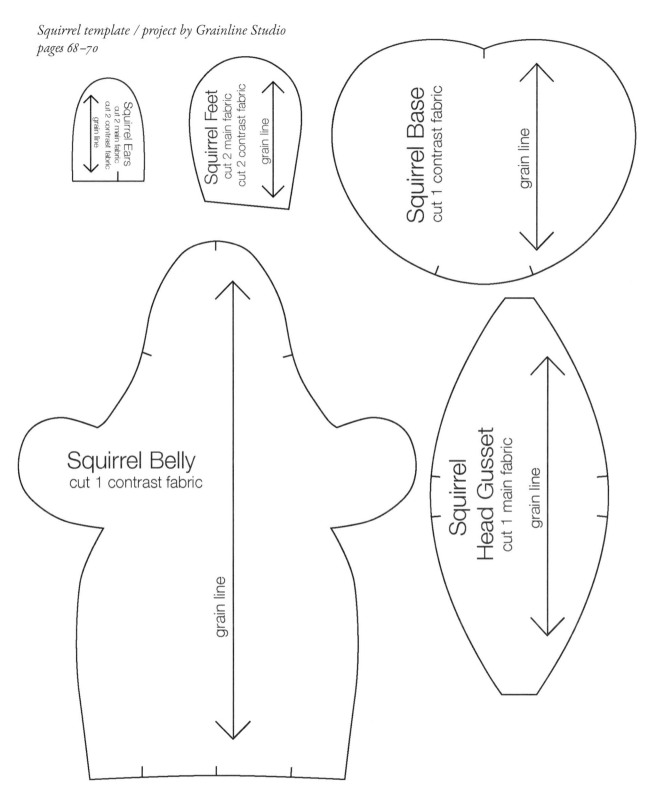

Squirrel Ears
cut 2 main fabric
cut 2 contrast fabric
grain line

Squirrel Feet
cut 2 main fabric
cut 2 contrast fabric
grain line

Squirrel Base
cut 1 contrast fabric
grain line

Squirrel Belly
cut 1 contrast fabric
grain line

Squirrel
Head Gusset
cut 1 main fabric
grain line

credits & thank you

dawn catanzaro & kristen tendyke / tech editors
cecily glowik macdonald / pattern grader
leila raabe / illustrator master
bristol ivy, lois johnson, and lily newton / proof readers
hannah & abe fettig / marketing & tech support

models
chloe, kate, taylor, imogen amelia, and sigrid sia

photography & graphic design
all photography* and layouts by carrie bostick hoge
except for:
• *Lori Ann Graham's Covered Journal tutorial on pgs 9–11*
• *Grainline Studio Squirrel tutorial images pgs 68*
• *Whitney Hayward for Twig & Horn Ad*
• *Purl Soho Ad*

chapter illustrations
by emily walker (instagram: fernsandfins)

thank you to all the contributors who have shared their talents with Making, No. 2 / FAUNA!

Please note these designs and patterns are for personal use only and not for resale or sharing.

Note: Sneak peek of a project collaboration between Grainline Studio & Madder, tunic on pages 94–95

Bear template / project pages 74–76

Fox tooth fairy pillow template / project pages 71–73

abbreviations

approx: approximately
beg: begin(ning)
BO: bind off
BOR: beginning of round
CC: contrast color
circ: circular
CO: cast on
cont: continue
dec('d): decrease(d)
dpns: double-pointed needles
est: establish(ed)
inc('d): increase(d)
k: knit
k1-f/b: Knit into front and back of next st (1 st increased).
k1-f/b/f: Knit into front, then back, then front again of next st (2 sts increased).
k1/L (left lifted increase): Pick up the left leg of the stitch two rows/rnds below the stitch just worked on RH needle and knit it (1 stitch increased).
k1/R (right lifted increase): Pick up the right leg of the stitch below the next stitch on LH needle and knit it, then knit the next stitch (1 stitch increased).
k1-tbl: Knit 1 through the back loop.
k2tog: Knit 2 sts together (1 st decreased).
k3tog: Knit 3 sts together (2 sts decreased).
LH: left hand
LN: left needle
m: marker
m1 (make 1): Insert LH needle from front to back under horizontal strand between st just worked and next st, knit lifted strand through the back loop (1 st increased).
m1-L: Insert LH needle from front to back under horizontal strand between st just worked and next st, knit lifted strand through the back loop (1 st increased).
m1-R: Insert LH needle from back to front under horizontal strand between st just worked and next st, knit lifted strand through the front loop (1 st increased).
meas: measure(s)
p: purl
patt: pattern

p1/R (right lifted increase): Pick up the right leg of the stitch below the next stitch on LH needle and purl it, then purl the next stitch (1 stitch increased, leans to the left on knit side).
p2tog: Purl 2 sts together (1 st decreased).
pc(s): piece(s)
pm: place marker
rem: remain
rep: repeat
rnd(s): round(s)
RH: right hand
RS: right side
sk2p: Slip 1 st knitwise to the RH needle; k2tog, then pass the slipped st over the st from k2tog (2 sts decreased).
sl: slip 1 st knitwise with yarn in front.
sl 1 wyif: Slip 1 st purlwise wyif.
sl 1 wyib: Slip 1 st purlwise wyib.
sl m: slip marker.
ssk (slip, slip, knit): Slip 2 sts one at a time knitwise to the RH needle; return sts to LH needle in turned position and knit them together through the back loops (1 st decreased).
st(s): stitch(es)
St st: stockinette stitch
tbl: through the back loop
WS: wrong side
wyib: with yarn in back
wyif: with yarn in front
yo: yarn over

stitches

Stockinette stitch flat
Knit on RS, purl on WS.

Stockinette stitch in the rnd
Knit every rnd.

Garter stitch flat
Knit every row.

Garter stitch in the rnd
Rnd 1: Purl.
Rnd 2: Knit.
Rep Rnds 1 and 2 for garter st in the rnd.

techniques

Backward loop cast on
*Wrap yarn around left thumb from front to back and secure in palm with other fingers. Insert needle upwards through strand on thumb. Slip loop from thumb onto RH needle, pulling yarn to tighten; rep from * for indicated number of sts.

Long tail cast on
www.knitty.com/ISSUEsummer05/FEATsum05TT.html

Provisional cast on
www.knitty.com/ISSUEfall05/FEATfall05TT.html

Crochet Provisional cast on
With waste yarn, beg with slipknot on crochet hook. *Wrap yarn around knitting needle counter-clockwise, then use crochet hook to draw yarn through loop on hook; rep from * for desired number of sts. Fasten off.

Alternating cable cast on
www.youtu.be/xphGoutbgq4

Cable cast on
Place a slipknot on LH needle and k1, slip new st onto LH needle; *insert RH needle between first 2 sts on LH needle, k1 from this position, leave the first st on LH needle and slip new st onto LH needle. Rep from * for desired number of sts.

I-cord
www.knittinghelp.com/video/play/i-cord-english

Kitchener stitch
www.knitty.com/ISSUEsummer04/FEATtheresasum04.html

Sunday Short Rows
www.sundayknits.com/techniques/shortrows.html

Three-needle bind off
Divide sts evenly over 2 needles; with the RS of garment pcs together (to form ridge on inside of garment), hold the needles parallel. With a third needle knit the first st of front and back needles together, *knit next st from each needle together,
(2 sts on RH needle), BO 1 st; rep from * until all sts are BO.

Tubular bind off
www.youtube.com/watch?v=FNbanlVzbxw&feature=youtu.be

Seaming
www.vogueknitting.com/pattern_help/how-to/beyond_the_basics/seaming

crochet
ch: chain
sk: skip
sl st: slip stitch
dc: double crochet
hdc: half double crochet
sc: single crochet

Crochet
www.crochet.org/?page=LearnToCrochet

pie recipe links
King Arthur Flour Sparkling White Sugar: www.kingarthurflour.com/shop/items/sparkling-white-sugar-15-oz

NY Cake – Leaf Fondant & Pie Cutter: www.nycake.com/leaves-fondant-and-pie-cutter-13808

EST · 2002

BROOKLYN

GENERAL

STORE

www.brooklyngeneral.com

· SPONSOR ·

· SPONSOR ·

Purl SOHO

CREATE | SHOP

www.purlsoho.com

FANCY TIGER CRAFTS
xxxxxxxxxx
www.fancytigercrafts.com

LYDIA'S FLOCK
ICELANDIC AND
SHETLAND FIBER

WWW.LYDIASFLOCK.COM

SUNDAY
knits

www.sundayknits.com

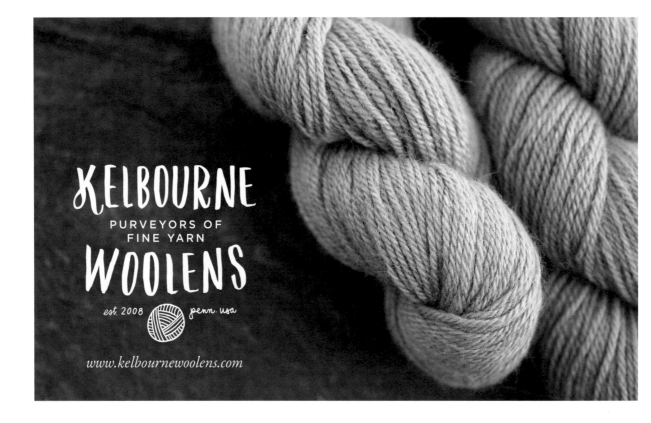

KELBOURNE
PURVEYORS OF
FINE YARN
WOOLENS

est. 2008 · penn. usa

www.kelbournewoolens.com

www.quinceandco.com

quince&co.

twig & horn

www.twigandhorn.com

GREEN
MOUNTAIN
SPINNERY

WWW.SPINNERY.COM

PortFiber

www.portfiber.com

LARS
Large Animal Research Station
QIVIUT SUPPLY
Fairbanks, Alaska
→ farmed muskox fiber ←

www.muskoxuaf.org

making

makingzine.com

Eden Cottage Yarns

LONDON
LOOP
www.loopknitting.com